RENELL
OF OAKENWALDT
AVENUE

Muriel Brooks

ISBN 978-1-63903-825-1 (paperback)
ISBN 978-1-63903-826-8 (digital)

Christian Faith Publishing
832 Park Avenue
Meadville, PA 16335
www.christianfaithpublishing.com

Though the narrative account in this book is factual the names of the characters have been changed for the purpose of confidentiality.

Printed in the United States of America

Renell of Oakenwaldt Avenue is dedicated to the loving memory of my parents, Dennis Calvin and Bennie Jean Allen, who are forever in my heart and thoughts. So many of life's valuable lessons I acquired from them.

To my brother, Elroy E. Allen (deceased), whom the family fondly called Peter. I miss him so much! He was not only my encourager, but one of my loudest cheerleaders. When Peter found out I was writing this book, he would ask, "Mimi, when will you finish the book and get it published? Am I in it?" Peter, I am so sorry you didn't get to read and enjoy this book, but yes, I included you in its pages. You will always be in my heart and thoughts! I love and miss you!

To all my family, friends and neighbors who lived on Oakenwaldt—each of you comprise a magnificent part of the "village" that has had such a lasting impact on my life.

Most of all, to my husband Robert "Bobby" Lewis Brooks and to our two adult sons, Robert (Rob) and Marc, for all your love and support. Your listening ears about my experiences and the peaks and valleys in my life on Oakenwaldt Avenue encouraged me to put pen to paper.

Contents

Acknowledgments

First of all, I want to thank and praise my Lord and Savior, Jesus Christ, for his unconditional love and how mindful he is of me! I am so appreciative of the numerous doors he has opened in my life as well as the doors he closed, doors which would have been detrimental had I entered them.

Thanks and appreciation to my husband, Robert, who is so proud of my book. Numerous nights I would ease out of bed to write precious memories of Oakenwaldt Avenue.

To my two loving and caring sons, Robert (Rob) and Marc, who have been so supportive of my desire to write Renell of Oakenwaldt Avenue. I now pass on the baton! My sincere desire is that you both pen your own childhood memories to share with your children.

To Yvonne-da Sherrie Copeland, my enthusiastic and vocal supporter, who was one of the main reasons I wrote *Renell of Oakenwaldt Avenue.* Thanks so much from my heart for your coaching and encouragement. Over twenty-five years ago, you encouraged me to write about life on Oakenwaldt Avenue after listening to me reminisce about both the fond and the traumatic memories that occurred in my close-knit community.

Special thanks to Frances Swinney, the wife of my pastor, Bishop Jerry Swinney, and the first lady of Bethel Christian Assembly, who prayed for me over twenty-five years ago and encouraged me to follow my heart and write. I expressed to her that I was ready to share some of my childhood experiences in book form, but at the time I was not motivated to devote myself to the task. It was only later that I felt God's prompting to complete this memoir. Lady Swinney, I finally got that nudge from God!

Winston Greene, whom we affectionately called (Tony),was more like a brother than a cousin, was a vibrate part of the exuberance, happiness and adventure on Oakenwaldt Avenue, Tony, you have consistently been a sounding board, a prayer partner, an encourager, a supporter and your caring nature knows no bounds. Thank you for taking time out of your busy schedule to reminisce, to share memories and for your invaluable assistance.

Lillian Douglas, my one and only sister, prayer partner, avid listener and unswerving supporter. Thanks for your unconditional love. I love and appreciate you dearly.

Carolyn Kirkland, a caring loving friend, and spiritual sister who would say, "Muriel, please finish your book! I am enjoying reading and visualizing the people of Oakenwaldt." Carolyn you were able to put a face to some of the Oakenwaldt village at my seventieth birthday celebration. Attendees are still talking about those scrumptious homemade egg rolls. Thank you so much for your prayers, encouragement, and helping hand.

Cheryl, Emma, and Mary, my lifelong friends of Oakenwaldt, I always love the times we can spend time together talking about the good old days. Emma, you have such a profound photographic memory of people and events that took place on Oakenwaldt over sixty-two years ago.

Thank you Jason Brown for how you masterfully captured the essence of Oakenwaldt Avenue in the 1950s as depicted on the cover of this book. Thank you for sharing your gift and talent.

1

Renell Adams of Oakenwaldt Avenue

To those who knew her, Renell Adams who lived on Oakenwaldt Avenue, Mansfield, Ohio, was a sensitive, perspicacious, little eight-year-old girl. But just like her unique street name, Oakenwaldt, Renell too was singularly special. Though friends and family often called her by such nicknames as *Mimi*, *Little Lady*, and *Miss Priss*, these labels only hinted at just a few of Renell's many innate qualities. While Renell's mother and some of Renell's friends and relatives called her *Mimi*, her older sister, Yvonne, referred to her as *Miss Priss*. This was because, as her sister explained, Renell acted so prissy or grown at times, especially when she dressed up to go to church. Still, other residents on Oakenwaldt Avenue called Renell *Miss Lady* because they said she had a mature, more adult mind and not the childlike mind of the typical eight-year-old.

Admittedly, Renell knew she was very inquisitive. She was always asking questions about what happened, how things happened, why they happened, and when they happened. Renell's questions seemed unquenchable and never ending. Not only did she have an excellent memory, but Renell made it her business to make certain that very little, if anything, got past her watchful eyes.

Renell considered Oakenwaldt Avenue an extraordinary, fun-filled street to live on, and she was elated to call it home. Everyone on the street—well, almost everyone—was warm, friendly, caring, and understanding. The adult residents on the street knew all the children by name, even if they would sometimes mistakenly call Renell and the other children by a sibling's name.

Actually, the more she thought about it, the more Renell realized that it wasn't such an oddity, since many children in the same family could pass as twins. In fact, even parents would, from time to time, call their own child by the wrong name. And yet as a child herself, Renell could not understand how an adult could mistake her for her sister Yvonne, but they did. Renell was actually much younger than her fifteen-year-old-sister, and she knew that though she and Yvonne were sisters, they bore no striking resemblance to each other.

On an almost daily basis, Renell would walk or run along Oakenwaldt Avenue. As she did so, neighbors would invariably call out to Renell and ask how she was doing. And without fail, she would always promptly respond, "I'm fine today, and how are you?" Then Renell would almost always glance up to find a familiar smile on the face of each greeter. Maybe that's why Renell felt so special.

Warm and tranquil feelings of deep contentment flooded Renell every time she thought about her street. Renell was genuinely happy to be an Oakenwaldter. She felt an unexplainable, but unwavering, loyalty to Oakenwaldt Avenue in Mansfield, Ohio, and staunchly believed that everyone in the world should live there. She sometimes wondered—not often, but every now and then—if other children felt the same way about their street as she felt about hers. Renell also experienced a similarly peaceful, serene feeling when she visited her grandmother who lived across town on Lily Street.

Evidently, Oakenwaldt must have been a strange name for a street because when Renell told people, especially grown-ups, where she lived, they would immediately ask her one of these three questions:

"You live where?"

"How do you pronounce or say your street name again?"

And usually, they would add, "How do you spell the name *Oakenwaldt*?"

Renell always assumed that such lines of questioning regarding the mere name of a street were overly exaggerated. She could understand those questions, had they come from a child who was baffled by the street name, but an adult! She thought adults were supposed to be smart and intelligent. Certainly her own parents asked questions of Renell, and of course, there was her nosy neighbor, Mrs. Monroe. And then too there were also teachers in her elementary school and Sunday school who asked Renell a host of questions. But Renell could understand such interrogation. Each of those individuals, with the exception of Mrs. Monroe, had a reason for asking their questions.

Yes, Renell had no doubt that adults must be super intelligent, maybe even brilliant. Why, they could answer just about anything she asked them! And, no wonder, she surmised! After all, they had lived a lot longer than her own brief eight years! However, with almost every passing day, as adult after adult proved Renell wrong and failed to have the answers the young girl sought, she was beginning to find her previous assumptions about adults to be a bit faulty. Renell just hoped that she herself would be a wise older person later in her own life.

Renell recalled that her grandmother had often reminded her, "Wisdom comes with age, child!" At least Renell thought that's what her grandmother Mama Jones said. But then, Renell inwardly surmised, just where was the "wisdom" of the adults who asked her all those monotonous questions about her street name? After all, Renell lived on Oakenwaldt Avenue, and she could both pronounce and spell it very well. It was not hard at all for her, and she was only eight years old!

Family

The Tie That Binds

As exciting as it was to live on Oakenwaldt Avenue, nothing filled Renell with as much joy as sentimental, affectionate thoughts of her family. Often when Renell thought of her family, she experienced warm, glowing feelings and, invariably, a broad, contagious smile brightened her countenance. To be an integral part of such a close, tightly knit family represented a wellspring of immense, indescribable happiness for Renell. She knew that she could, without fail, always count on her family's enduring bonds of sharing, caring, giving, forgiving, and loving. To Renell, the harmony, trust, and deep feeling of security she sensed within her family seemed to engulf the little girl like a warm, thick, cozy blanket.

Renell's family was also experiencing an overwhelming time of sadness, questioning the *why*, despair, and hopelessness since the sudden, unexpected death of her brother Donald. Donald had expired the year before, at the young tender age of sixteen, from a car accident. The entire family was devastated by that tragedy.

Renell's father, Dennis Adams, was a compassionate, generous, loving, and soft-spoken man who nonetheless worked with relentless drive and energy to support his family. He held a full-time position at the Westinghouse Electric Corporation, a factory that made and sold household appliances. As an African American entrepreneur Mr. Adams and his uncle also owned a hauling business. Respected and admired by the residents on Oakenwaldt Avenue, neighbors would sometime remark, "Wow, Mr. Adams always has a smile on his face. He is such a hardworking man who takes good care of his family and will do whatever he can to help."

Mr. Adams consistently instilled in his six children that they were family and that they were to always help one another achieve their dreams, that they were to always support one another, and, most of all, that they were to always love one another. Mr. Adams would often remind Renell and her siblings, "When one goes up, we all go up. Pray and look out for one another." And he would further admonish Renell and her siblings, "Don't let anyone hurt your brother or sister," and would also wisely add, "Don't start a fight, but treat others as you would like to be treated."

Renell's mother, Bennie Jean Adams, was not only beautiful but was a loving, caring, and extraordinary woman of God. A firm disciplinarian, Mrs. Adams stated her instructions to her children only once and she did not repeat them. They knew she meant business, and whoever broke the rule or rules would face consequences. Each child knew and understood the household rules as well as the subsequent ramifications of their decisions if their mother's rules were not followed. The Adams children dared not defy or upset their mother.

While an unquestionably firm disciplinarian, Mrs. Adams showered her children with hugs and kisses. She expressed daily how much she loved each of them, and continuously encouraged their unique talents and abilities. Mrs. Adams also excelled as a superb cook and was a fastidious housekeeper. Everything in the Adams home was organized, so much so that Renell knew, with unbridled confidence, that she could literally eat off any floor in the house if she wanted to!

On a daily basis, the Adams children were required to keep their rooms immaculate. Additionally, Mrs. Adams ensured that each child had their own, daily assigned chores. Each night before retiring to bed, the family tidied up. Like clockwork, every Saturday was the designated day of the week when all the Adams children worked in unison. They worked together mopping the house, dusting the furniture, and washing the baseboards and walls.

"We never know who will stop by to visit. Our house is a reflection of who we are," Mrs. Adams often wisely remarked. She would further admonish, "Cleanliness is next to godliness, and we will keep this house clean and everything will be in its assigned place."

Every one of the Adams children knew their mother meant what she said, and it was not difficult for them to comply with her rules. Mrs. Adams always guided her children and her household with a winning combination of both firmness and love. And at any time that guests and neighbors entered the Adams home, they always felt a cordial welcome and the presence of God.

Each morning after the children made their beds and dressed, the family gathered in the living room for family devotions. Devotions began with singing songs from a red hymnal, accompanied by Renell's older brother, Lewis, on the piano. The family then would pray together for about fifteen minutes. After the family prayer ended, each child quoted a Bible verse they either learned from their home Bible reading or from Sunday school. Finally, the family ate a big breakfast that Mrs. Adams prepared for them. Then off to school, the children went. During the summer months, the Adams children followed the same routine. On hot summer days, after they completed their devotions and morning chores, instead of going to school, they were allowed to go outside to play with their many friends on Oakenwaldt Avenue.

In addition to maintaining a spotless home and cooking delicious, mouthwatering meals, Mrs. Adams loved to sew, crochet and knit and to lovingly decorate her home. Mrs. Adams made curtains for the windows of the family home as well as tablecloths for the kitchen table. Renell enjoyed setting the table for the family's dinner each evening on the beautiful tablecloths her mother sewed.

Mrs. Adams also sewed beautiful clothes for her two daughters. Renell loved the feel and texture of the soft and silky blue gorgeous angora sweater and skirt that Mrs. Adams had so skillfully knitted for Christmas. When Renell wore the stunning outfit to church for the first time, all eyes were on her. It was so meticulously tailored that people quickly assumed that Mrs. Adams must have purchased it at a high-end store in either Columbus or Cleveland, Ohio. Instead, it had been lovingly knitted by Renell's mother, Mrs. Adams, who took pride in everything she did!

For Mrs. Adams, every task, every undertaking had to be completed with excellence. Renell's mother also crocheted fancy doilies which she washed, starched, and ironed. The doilies stood up, stiff from the starch, in a decorative design. Mrs. Adams would place the doilies on the coffee and end tables and carefully then place the lamps with decorative shades and other figurines on them. Mrs. Adams also enjoyed making her home a centerpiece of ornate beauty and charm for her family to enjoy. She endeavored to pass on to each of her children that same approach in caring for the family home and everything in it. Renell recalled, however, that it took her young brother, Steven, several attempts to grasp the importance of caring for their home. Steven loved going outdoors to play games and kickball. However, his disobedience and repeated failure to complete his chores resulted in several spankings and restrictions from outdoor play before he finally understood.

The siblings knew their mother was a prayer warrior, a visionary, and an ardent supporter for each one of her children. During prayer time, she always asked the Lord to protect her children, guide them to make good decisions, and give each one an obedient spirit. Her prayers were always longer for Steven.

Periodically, Mrs. Adams reminded each of her offspring of their life's mission and calling. As if she could see into the future, Mrs. Adams would wisely and knowingly tell Renell and her siblings, "Each of you will have to work hard to achieve in this world. I am preparing you to become self-sufficient and productive citizens. By applying yourselves to succeed and asking the Lord for His help and guidance, you can be anything that you set your minds to be." Then each time after those profound statements left her lips, Mrs. Adams would invariably recite the same jingle that Renell soon learned by heart, "Good, better, best! Never let it rest! Until the good is better and the better is best!"

Even at the tender age of eight years old, Renell understood this message and held her mother's proverb dear to her heart! Renell memorized it, and each time Mrs. Adams would recite the adage aloud to Renell and to her brothers and sister, Renell would say it silently to herself.

Lewis Adams, Renell's oldest brother, was a conscientious and studious young man. She remembered the big celebration that the family had when he graduated from Mansfield Senior High. Mr. and Mrs. Adams were so proud of Lewis and all his academic accomplishments. It was a sad day in the Adams home when he left for college in September. The family was going to miss Lewis so much, but Lewis was so excited to go to Central State College in Wilberforce, Ohio. After he went off to college, Lewis would call each week and would send the family letters. Renell was so excited when he would come home from college on break. She loved to hear him play the piano and she would listen very attentively when he shared stories of his college life and friends. Many of his new friends came to college from different states and that excited Renell. She would run and get the *World Book Encyclopedia* and find information about that particular state. She would find out the climate, population, and interesting places to visit. She was getting her questions ready when some of his friends would come to their house on college breaks to visit.

Renell believed that Lewis's dream of becoming a certified public accountant would come true. With each passing year of college, the family celebrated Lewis's academic accomplishments; and at the start of each new school year, the family would take Lewis back to college and help him settle into his dorm.

Lewis's time away at college each year sounded so exciting. Renell knew it would not be long before her sister, Yvonne, would leave for college. She genuinely loved, adored, and looked up to her sister as a role model. She thought her sister was so pretty and had the cutest dimples. Yvonne was soft-spoken, smart, conscientious, caring, kind, a thinker, and an observer. She had patience with Renell and her little friends. Daily, Yvonne would spend quality time reading her Bible and praying as well as doing her schoolwork and chores around the house. She was the epitome of a Spirit-filled saved teenage young lady that loved the Lord with her whole heart. Yvonne was actively involved in the church's various activities and auxiliaries, and she enjoyed spending quality time with friends from church.

Another saying from their mother was "birds of a feather flocked together". Mrs. Adams wanted her children to primarily associate with children from the church because she believed they were taught and practiced the same biblical principles.

Yvonne only wanted the best for her little sister, but at times, Renell would test the limits of her older sister with her incessant, time-consuming questions. She would say to Renell, "Priss, where did you come from?" Though Yvonne loved Renell very much, she needed a break from her eight-year-old sister. Resignedly, Renell would obey when her sister redirected her, only because she was taught to listen to her older siblings. Renell did not like to do so, but she did not want to get into trouble with her parents.

Yvonne loved going to Lily Street to visit her grandmother and her aunts and to spend time with her cousin Sharon. Yvonne was the babysitter for one of her aunt's alumnus from Wilberforce College, who was also an attorney. Yvonne diligently saved her money from her babysitting jobs.

The residents on Oakenwaldt Avenue always spoke highly of Yvonne, and they expected her to achieve in any given task that was assigned to her and to be successful in the profession of her choice. One of Yvonne's closest friend, Rita, lived on Oakenwaldt Avenue and also attended the same church as the Adams.

Renell's brother, Eugene was six years older than her. He was a devoted athlete who played several different sports at school. A basketball court was located in the back of the Newman Elementary School which was on Oakenwaldt Avenue and often was the site of numerous ball games for Eugene and the other neighborhood boys. As an outstanding basketball player, Eugene and the other neighborhood boys were very competitive. If allowed to do so, Eugene would stay on the court all day and night. Eugene enjoyed the attention, as the girls on the street cheered the boys on. Sometimes, when the ball did not go into the basket or if their team was losing, Renell would hear words come out of the mouths of Eugene and the other boys playing on the court that would really get them in trouble.

Renell knew without a doubt that Eugene loved to eat and that he could eat a mixing bowl full of crunched-up cornflakes, splattered with several tablespoons of sugar and filled to the brim of the large bowl with milk. He also loved syrup sandwiches so much that Renell said, "Just made me sick to know that he could eat that." Eugene was allowed to eat as much as he liked, but only if his eyes were not bigger than his belly. In other words he was not allowed to throw away food. He was to get only what he could eat.

Eugene would ask Renell why she asked so many questions. He would sometimes call her nosy, and she would curtly reply, "If you want to know something, you should ask!" And so, that is what she did.

Once, Renell's grandmother told Renell that she could become an outstanding lawyer like Perry Mason, to which Eugene sarcastically responded, "She would be a better detective like Encyclopedia Brown or Nancy Drew because she is always asking questions and investigating!"

Steven, Renell's younger brother, was just one year and one week younger than Renell. While he was an intelligent and inquisitive boy, he was also very mischievous. He enjoyed reading many different kinds of books, like the family's World Book Encyclopedias. The superhero comic books and his favorite two characters Superman and Batman intrigued him.

Often, in the house, Steven would tie a towel or remnants of fabrics around his neck and jump off kitchen chairs and the upstairs steps, pretending he could fly in the air like Superman. When he was caught doing that, he was reprimanded and reminded that he could seriously hurt himself. When he would get ready to go outside to play with his cape on, Mrs. Adams would remind him that Superman was just a fictional character and he could not really fly. She would say, "Steven, do not jump off of any neighbor's high steps or jump out of any tree limbs because you cannot fly!" Being a defiant little boy, Steven would do both.

Steven also loved to take things apart and put them back together again. He could replace every bolt, screw, and nail back in its original place. Neighbors, when they bought items that required assembly, would ask if Steven could help them. He loved the challenge, and the majority of the time, he was successful. The neighbors nick-named him The Fixer. His aunt, whom he called Auntie, would say, "Steven has the ability to become a mechanical engineer."

Steven would reply, "If they make a lot of money, I might consider that for a career."

Obviously proud of her son's accomplishments, Mrs. Adams would beam and remark, "That Steven can be a handful!"

Steven remembered all the Bible stories taught to him at home and in Sunday school, but he never enjoyed hearing references to the lake of fire and to the devil. Clearly frustrated, he would ask his Sunday school teacher, "Why do you always bring those two frightful subjects up constantly?"

In response, his Sunday school teacher would patiently tell Steven, "I want to inform you that the lake of fire is a place you will be going to if you continue to be disobedient and not listen to your parents and adults."

Clearly not appeased by the Sunday school teacher's explanation, one day Steven got the bold idea to dig a hole in the backyard and find the devil and kill him. Unbeknownst to the family, Steven would, on a daily basis, go outside in the backyard and dig and dig until one day, his father, Mr. Adams, stumbled upon Steven intently digging a deep hole in the ground.

Mr. Adams questioned Steven about all the dirt that was on the grass, to which Steven unabashedly stated, "Dad, I am digging in the ground to find the devil, and I am going to kill him."

At first, Mr. Adams was upset as he gazed at the large hole in his yard. But then, slowly he began to smile and then to laugh. "Son," Mr. Adams patiently began as he gently placed his hand on his young son's shoulder, "you will never find the devil in the ground." Mr. Adams went on to explain to his son that the devil is a spirit.

Well, that explanation ignited further questions and multiple conversations, too numerous to mention here and even more than Renell herself customarily asked.

Renell's family was one of several families that had relatives who also resided on Oakenwaldt Avenue. Mrs. Adams' sister, Inell, her husband, Winston, and their two-year-old son, Tony, lived down the street, directly across Newman School. Renell, her siblings, and cousins all called their aunt Auntie while they referred to their uncle as Uncle Winston.

Auntie and Uncle Winston were like the Adams children's second parents, and so Tony was more like a baby brother than their cousin. Renell enjoyed playing with Tony and pulling his fat, chubby two-year-old frame around in his favorite red wagon. Even at the tender age of two years old, he could clearly instruct Renell to continue pulling his wagon and she would readily comply. If she would go too slowly, Tony would tell her, "Go faster, faster." Everyone spoiled Tony. He was exceptionally smart, and even as a toddler, he did not forget a face.

Auntie was the first black social worker in Mansfield. Not only did she specialize in working with the aging population, but she was also a Notary, a Wilberforce Alumnae, member of the Mansfield NAACP, and a dedicated supporter, and committed member of Mitchell Chapel AME Church. The residents on Oakenwaldt Avenue admired and respected her as did the other residents in Mansfield, Ohio, did. Others often sought her for advice on numerous topics.

Auntie's job fascinated Renell. She enjoyed accompanying her aunt on house calls, especially during the summers. Though never discussed, Renell detected an unspoken stigma attached to the vocation of social worker. Those individuals who chose this career field were often perceived as nosy and uncaring individuals who did not want their clients to possess comfortable things in their homes. Renell heard that if a client possessed modern conveniences, then that individual did not require help from the state. Yet Renell knew firsthand that Auntie was not like that. Her aunt would always ensure that her clients had enough food and that their utilities such as electricity, gas, and water functioned properly. Yes, Renell concluded, her aunt was definitely the right person for the job. Auntie loved her job, and she was passionate to make sure that her clients were taken good care of.

Auntie's husband, Uncle Winston was a barber. As an entrepreneur and one of the town's few, licensed, African American barbers, he not only owned his own barber shop, but Renell's uncle also employed several barbers and a shoe shiner. The shoe shiner would clean and spit shine shoes for his customers. Under his tutelage, he also trained and supervised intern barbers who provided grooming services to Uncle Winston's patrons.

While Uncle Winston's barbershop was closed every Thursday, he worked every other day of the week except Sundays. Saturdays at the barbershop were always very busy because those who worked during the week would want to get their hair cut on Saturday and catch up on some of the week's gossip. Uncle Winston was a very organized person who did things in a precise and organized matter. Every Thursday, Uncle Winston's day away from the barbershop, he mowed, weeded and manicured his family's yard. He had beautiful, rich, thick grass. After mowing the yard, Uncle Winston would take care of personal business and also complete the honey-do list left by his wife. A superb cook, Uncle Winston often bragged about his teacher—his mom— who taught him how to cook so well. Born in Selma, Alabama, Uncle Winston grew up on a farm. His mother not only taught the young boy and his siblings how to cook, but she also taught them how to sew as well. Uncle Winston fried the best hot crunchy fish and home fires and Renell felt that her uncle's homemade, delectable ice cream should have been served in the finest restaurants. Uncle Winston and several of his American Legion buddies would go on a fishing trip each year to Canada. There, they would catch an abundance of various kinds of fish. Uncle Winston also enjoyed hunting trips with Renell's father, Mr. Adams, in which they would catch rabbits, squirrels and deer.

Mrs. Adams's brother, John, his wife, Marlene, and their daughter, Deanna, also resided on Oakenwaldt Avenue. Deanna and Renell were born on the same cold day in January. They were also in the same classes in Newman School. Renell and Deanna would walk to and from school together.

Mama Jones, Mrs. Adams' mother, did not live on Oakenwaldt Avenue, but she was known to just about everyone on the street. They would often see her driving her black and yellow Buick to visit the Adams family. Though she lived on Lily Street, Mama Jones, too, was also an African American entrepreneur in Mansfield. She owned a neighborhood store on Lily Street, and Renell and other family members would work in the store on weekends and during the summer. Renell had several family members who also lived on Lily Street.

3

A Village of "Oakenwaldters"

Oakenwaldters, as the residents on Oakenwaldt Avenue fondly referred to themselves, had many things in common that bonded their close-knit neighborhood even more closely together. Renell supposed that the best way to describe Oakenwaldters would be to compare them to a huge melting pot. On Oakenwaldt Avenue, many diverse, ethnic groups lived together, unabashedly sharing their distinct culture, food, and customs with each other. In short, Oakenwaldt Avenue represented a multicultural, multiethnic synthesis of blacks, whites, interracial families, and Native Americans harmoniously coexisting in the twenty-five or so houses that line their unique street. On any given evening, a passerby might smell the aroma of bratwurst sizzling on a stove from the Mayer's home. Or the aroma of pork chops, greens, sweet potatoes, and sweet cornbread would linger in the air from the Adams' home.

Pork chops were one of Renell's favorite meats. Every Friday evening, the smell of hot, freshly cooked, fried fish emanated from majority of the twenty-five homes on Oakenwaldt Avenue and permeated the street air. And every Friday, Renell's nostrils and palate relished the myriad types of fish and the distinct taste and smell of each. Some of the Oakenwaldters would serve fish and grits for their evening meal, while others would include entrées of coleslaw and green beans with their unique fish recipes. Mr. Jones, who lived on the corner of Oakenwaldt and Vine Street, would barbeque ribs and sell dinners in his yard. Wow, the tantalizing smells would simply make Renell's mouth water! Occasionally Mr. Adams would purchase a slab for the family. Yummy ribs with the best barbeque sauce on the sliced bread. Mrs. Adams would serve baked beans and corn on the cob. Such good eating on those nights! Renell would always want another piece of those delicious, mouthwatering barbeque ribs later in the evening as a snack before brushing her teeth and going to bed.

As a tight-knit community, several Oakenwaldters attended the same church, while others on the street shared no religious affiliation or common culture but, rather, were related by blood. Some were fishing buddies, while still others worked together at one of the many factories in town.

One undeniable common thread, however, was that all the elementary-aged children who lived on Oakenwaldt attended Newman School. While the front of the school rested on Central Avenue, the school's baseball field, its jungle gyms, and its basketball courts were all located in the back of Newman School, right on Oakenwaldt Avenue. Such a convenient location provided quick access to a fun-filled time of play for Renell and the other children in the neighborhood.

The saying "It takes a village to raise a child" must have originated on Oakenwaldt Avenue if, for no other reason than that the majority of the adults who lived on the street looked out for the welfare of *all* the children on Oakenwaldt. Of the twenty-five homes on the street, at least twenty-three of them had two or more children.

Despite no established neighborhood watch program, Renell experienced constant indescribable feelings of safety and protection as a resident of Oakenwaldt Avenue. Though never officially verbalized, the residents on Oakenwaldt Avenue felt it was their duty and responsibility to not only look out for the other residents, but for the family members and possessions of those residents as well. She knew that caring eyes were always peering from windows and were watching who was coming and who was going on the street. Doors of the homes that lined Oakenwaldt Avenue were not just opened to circulate fresh air, but it seemed to Renell that concerned eyes peered behind the doors and through the windows and were ever watching and observing every occurrence on the street.

Renell had no doubt that she would be promptly reprimanded by an adult if they saw her do anything they perceived to be inappropriate. There was not a day that went by that a child was not reprimanded by an adult on Oakenwaldt Avenue.

Gee whiz, all I want to do is have some fun! Renell often thought to herself.

The activities that Renell and her playmates chose were not bad. Admittedly, however, Renell justified any questionable actions on her part, noting that it was all done in the name of fun!

To Renell, Oakenwaldt Avenue was so safe that it seemed to her that keys were only needed to start the cars. Doors were rarely locked on Oakenwaldt, except at night or if families went away on vacations. Renell was confident that trust was evident on Oakenwaldt Avenue. She often wondered to herself that if doors were locked by the residents, how could the Borden milkman deliver their milk and put it in their refrigerator? Yes, right in their refrigerator! Wow, that is *trust!*

Like the milkman, the mailman also personally knew all the residents of Oakenwaldt by name, and he would stop at certain homes during his walk to chat or sip a cool cup of water. He would also catch up on the street's gossip. As a result of his daily mail deliveries, the mailman knew when important events occurred. He would occasionally bring treats to the dogs on the street. Yes, on Oakenwaldt Avenue, even the four-pawed creatures were friends to the milkman and to the mailman!

Indeed, many close and lasting friendships were developed on Oakenwaldt. In fact, some friendships were even closer than those of blood relatives within the same family. The women would either stand in front of their homes or sit on their porches chatting with one another while watching the children play. Renell felt that the wives and mothers wisely used their time to catch up on the latest happenings on the street.

Sometimes, when playtime activities were not as noisy and boisterous as at other times, the children would hear some of the laughter and discussions that their elders shared. Though they knew better than to repeat what they heard, they would steal knowing glances and quietly laugh together later about what they had heard.

Maria and Jennifer Dock were close friends of Renell and attended the same church as the Adams family. Mrs. Rene Dock was a nurse at Mansfield General Hospital, but Renell called her Sister Dock because adults at her church used the title Sister or Brother before their first or last name. Maria and Jennifer's father, Mr. Dock, worked at one of the many factories in town.

Renell loved to visit the Dock's home. It was such a relaxing and spiritual atmosphere. Renell had the best time playing with the sisters in the backyard in the dollhouse their father had constructed for them. Renell enjoyed listening to Maria and Jennifer practice on their piano the songs that had been assigned to them by their music teacher for the week. They also enjoyed skillfully playing their musical tunes for the children on the street.

Maria and Jennifer would pretend to be Renell's music teacher, and they would tell Renell that she had done an outstanding job on the songs they taught her, but they failed to remember that the Adams family also had a piano, that Renell's sister and brother had previously taken piano lessons and that Renell was waiting on her time to do so as well. Maria and Jennifer told her their teacher would tap their knuckles if they made a mistake. Once Maria warned Renell she would have to submit to that self-same punishment if she made a mistake on the piano. They both laughed because Renell knew she was imitating her teacher. Maria knew if either she or Jennifer would tap Renell's fingers, Renell would tap them right back. Instinctively, Renell knew how to protect herself. Her brothers enjoyed wrestling and they taught her a few moves. She was a girl who could defend herself, and Maria knew that!

Across the street from the Dock's home lived another of Renell's close friends, Erma Johnson. Erma lived with her grandmother, Sister Rose, and her uncle. Erma and her grandmother also attended the same church as the Adams family. Erma's grandmother was a person who took everything she heard literally. Renell always knew that everyone would burst out laughing moments after Sister Rose began to speak.

For instance, a Maxwell House Coffee commercial would come on the television each day to advertise its product. Though the television commercial was a bit far-fetched, Sister Rose believed everything she heard regarding it. Without fail, the coffee pot on the commercial would always make a singing noise after it was placed on the hot stove. As the commercial ended, the words "good to the last drop" would repetitively sound to a lively musical jingle. Soon after, Sister Rose would remark, "I bought that coffee and my coffeepot has never sang a song like that, and they should stop coming on the television lying about the singing coffee pot."

At that point, Renell and Erma would knowingly look at each other and burst out in laughter. For what seemed like hours, they would laugh uncontrollably at Sister Rose's comment. Every time they would look at each other, they would burst out in spontaneous laughter again. Sister Rose was serious, and she did not appreciate the fact that the girls considered her observations funny, but the two girls found the older woman's comments hilarious.

Renell and Erma tried to patiently explain to Sister Rose that commercials were only on television to persuade the public to purchase the advertised product and that the commercial helped pay for the television airtime. They went on to explain that Sister Rose played right into the sponsor's hand when she purchased their product. The girls explained that Sister Rose and other should simply just enjoy the commercials on the television and to think of them solely as entertainment. Sister Rose eventually relented, stating, "Maybe I should listen to what you both are saying, and I will keep more money in my pocketbook."

Renell had learned firsthand about the deception of television advertising. The previous Christmas, Renell's mother had warned Renell and her younger brother Steven that they would inevitably view many commercials advertising toys during the upcoming Thanksgiving and Christmas season. Renell's mother wisely cautioned them not to start asking for everything they saw on the television because she and Mr. Adams would not be purchasing those items. Besides, Mrs. Adams added, "All the toys are not as they appear in the television advertisements."

Renell knew her mother always told the truth and that her mother was simply passing the truth on to her children.

Right next door to the Dock's, on their right side, lived another one of Renell's close friends, Sherry Grant. Most of the time, Sherry and Renell were inseparable. In fact, Renell loved Sherry just like the little sister she never had. Renell was a year older than Sherry. If two girls were compatible, it was Sherry and Renell. When Oakenwaldters saw one girl, the other one was usually not far behind.

Sherry Grant had a head full of long, thick, coarse, coal-black hair. It was the prettiest head of hair of any child that Renell knew. Yvonne, Renell's sister, would often comb Sherry's hair for Mrs. Grant. Mrs. Grant would comment and say, "Sherry's hair is long like mine, but it is not straight, and she needed help with combing it." Yvonne would comb and brush it to get out all the tangles. Sherry was a little tender headed and she would cry, but when her hair was finally plaited into two long braids, she looked like a beautiful Indian princess.

Sherry's father was biracial, and her mother was a Blackfoot Indian. Mrs. Grant's hair was also long and coal black, and she had a pretty long, narrow face. Often, Mrs. Grant would wear her hair plaited in one long braid. Sherry had high cheekbones, the most gorgeous dark brown eyes, and rich olive-colored skin. Sometimes Mrs. Grant would tell Renell and Sherry stories about her family, culture, and customs. Because Mrs. Grant's experiences were so divergent from their own, the two girls would laugh at some things Mrs. Grant would say. Renell loved to hear stories about people's lives and their family relationships. Her own grandmother would relate many stories to the girls about her life as a young girl growing up. Renell often said that one day she would indeed tell her own children about her childhood days as well.

Not everyone on Oakenwaldt Avenue was cordial and friendly. Renell recalled memories of one of those not so friendly families, the Mayers. It was not the entire family, just the father. Renell remembered that the Mayers, who were German, would prepare bratwurst and serve them on soft rolls.

Renell recalled Mrs. Mayer stating, "In Germany, bratwursts were eaten on hard rolls called brotchen. My children enjoyed eating brotchen rolls until they went to school in America and tasted the soft rolls. Now my children prefer the soft rolls, and that is only what they really want to eat."

Renell loved the bratwurst prepared by Mrs. Mayer. The dish reminded her of the delicious sausage her grandmother would serve for breakfast when she spent the night there. Wow, they were so delicious with her homemade biscuits!

The Mayers lived in the last house nearest to the school on the right side of the street. The majority of the children in the neighborhood could only visit their house when Mr. Mayer was at work. By three o'clock every weekday afternoon, the crowd of children would disperse.

Mr. Mayer did not mind letting all the children know that he did not particularly care for Negroes. He stated, "In Germany I never saw Negroes until World War II, and I do not want my children around them." Mr. Mayer would have died and turned over in his grave had he known that his own children were in the Negro children's home playing, and that the Negro children were in his home and yard. Most of the children's parents on Oakenwaldt would tell their offspring that Mr. Mayer just needed Jesus and much prayer. Mr. Mayer was Renell's first encounter with racism and prejudice.

Renell's father, Mr. Adams, patiently explained to his children that there were all kinds of people in the world and only ignorant people failed to realize that God made everyone as he wanted them to look. Renell realized it was her duty to love everyone as it is written in the Bible, regardless of their color, creed or culture. Renell's father never spoke negatively about Mr. Mayer, but only told his children that he was praying for Mr. Mayer and had asked God to change Mr. Mayer's heart. Despite Mr. Mayer's prejudicial attitudes, his children and all the other children on Oakenwaldt Avenue got along well. Renell never knew if her father's prayers were ever answered because later, Mr. Mayer and his family moved to another community in Mansfield that was predominantly German.

4

Mrs. Busybody, Mr. Grump and other Neighbors

Oakenwaldt Avenue would not have been complete without a resident busybody. Unfortunately, the street's foremost busybody lived right next door to Renell's family, on their left side. Because this person actually knew the when, where, how, what, and why about everything, Renell always considered her the unofficial founder and director of the neighborhood watch. Her name was Mrs. Monroe. Renell knew firsthand Ms. Monroe to be a mean-spirited, irascible old woman.

Because Mrs. Monroe knew the exact time when neighbors came home or when they left their homes each morning, the residents on Oakenwaldt Avenue wondered if Mrs. Monroe ever slept. Renell and the other children all knew of Mrs. Monroe's insatiable curiosity, because they would observe her always staring openly and unabashedly up and down the street from one of the windows of her home.

Renell found Mrs. Monroe to seldom be in a good mood and to always exhibit strange peculiarities. At least it seemed strange to the children on Oakenwaldt Avenue to see Mrs. Monroe sitting on her front porch swinging and shamelessly smoking a pipe for all to see. The children assumed that only men smoked pipes! True enough, Renell conceded, she and the other children did observe some women on the street who smoked cigarettes in their yards or on their porch, but never had they witnessed a lady openly smoke a pipe—that is, until they saw Mrs. Monroe!

Renell and the other children on Oakenwaldt Avenue knew Mrs. Monroe made it her business to know the business of anyone who lived on Oakenwaldt Avenue. In fact, Mrs. Monroe felt it her civic duty and responsibility to know everything about everybody. Renell instinctively knew that if Mrs. Monroe observed her or any other child doing anything that they were not supposed to do, it would not be a secret for long. Mrs. Monroe would immediately report her finding to the parents of the alleged perpetrators.

Daily, Mrs. Monroe rhythmically moved back and forth on her porch swing, smoking her pipe. Renell already knew that Mrs. Monroe was seldom, if ever, in a good mood. However, having been taught to always be polite, Renell and the other children would speak to Mrs. Monroe and greet her with "Hello, good morning [or good afternoon]. How are you doing?"

Mrs. Monroe would then inevitably reply with her classic response, "I do dis declare, my anklets, and my riskets, and my joints are hurting. I got pain and misery up and down my legs. I tan't a bit a good." Without fail, every time, Mrs. Monroe would respond with those words; and Renell, upon hearing them, would laugh uncontrollably. It was just so funny to Renell that Mrs. Monroe would say the same identical words over and over again.

Renell concluded that Mrs. Monroe's most blatant idiosyncrasy was probably her pipe smoking. Renell knew that one day, when she mustered up enough nerve, she was going to ask Mrs. Monroe why she smoked a pipe. After all, Renell mused, Mrs. Monroe herself was really the only person who could honestly answer that question, wasn't she? Renell had already asked her parents, but they did not know why Mrs. Monroe smoked a pipe. Besides, reasoned Renell, her dad had often said, "If you want to know something about someone, get it straight from the horse's mouth." Though Renell knew he was not referring to the question she wanted to ask Mrs. Monroe, Renell felt justified that his advice just might apply in this case.

So on one particular day, when Mrs. Monroe was swinging on her front porch and smoking her pipe, she saw Renell and struck up a conversation with her. Specifically, the older lady quizzed Renell regarding some visitors who came to their house on the previous evening.

Mrs. Monroe began by asking, "Who were those folks with the Michigan license plates over to your house last night?" Renell explained that the visitors were her cousins from Detroit. Mrs. Monroe then remarked, "I see," and continued her questioning. "Are they your father's people or your mother's people?"

By this time, Renell secretly surmised that Mrs. Monroe was really being nosy, but she dared not openly say that to her elderly, inquisitive neighbor. Instead, Renell politely responded that they were her father's first cousins. Mrs. Monroe was not aware, but Renell's cousin Daffey had already informed Renell that Mrs. Monroe had come outside on her porch when Daffey and her family first drove up that previous evening.

Daffey had previously explained to Renell, "In Detroit, people mind their own business or they might get shot. Your neighbor is mighty bold to come out and just look people up and down." Daffey had then wondered aloud to Renell if Mrs. Monroe might be a little crazy. Renell understood her cousin's concerns and she explained to Daffey that Mrs. Monroe was just a very, very nosy neighbor who felt it was her job to dig up the facts on everyone and everything on Oakenwaldt Avenue.

That particular day, since Mrs. Monroe had asked Renell several questions, Renell thought it was only fitting and proper to, in turn, ask Mrs. Monroe at least one question. Renell realized that she might get in deep trouble, but after all, it was only one question.

So Renell asked Mrs. Monroe the one question that had long lingered in her mind, "Mrs. Monroe, why do you smoke a pipe instead of cigarettes?"

Mrs. Monroe promptly replied to the little girl's query, explaining that "I don't like cigarettes 'cuz they's is too small to hold. When I's wuz a little girl, I would watch my daddy smoke his pipe. My daddy's 'joyment in da evenings often centered on his smokin' his pipe. I enjoyed watching my daddy smoke his pipe, and I secretly loved duh smell of da pipe's tobacco."

In a rare talkative mood, Mrs. Monroe continued and said, "One summer's evening, my daddy and I, we wuz sitting on the front porch of our home just thinkin' on the happenins' of our day. As usual, my daddy wuz smokin' his pipe. My momma wuz in the house doin some house cleaning, and soon, she called Daddy in to help her. So's my daddy lays down his pipe an' goes in our house to help Momma. Whiles my daddy wuz gone, the smell from his pipe wuz so strong. I had always wanted to take me's a puff, and now wuz my chance. I wanted to find out why smokin' a pipe brought my daddy so much pleasure."

"So's I picks up my daddy's pipe and begins to puff on it. But it wuz more than I could handle at the time. I starts coughin', and then I begins to feel dizzy. When Daddy comes back on the porch, I thinks up an excuse to go inside the house. I often wunder if my daddy knew what I done. As soons as I enters the house, I runs to my room and falls face down on my bed. I wuz out like a light as soon as my head hits duh pillow."

"Though I didn't like the taste of the pipe at first, I knew that as I got older, I wuz going to smoke me a pipe just like my daddy. Cuz' if it wuz good enough for my daddy and brought such pleasure to him, I felt it would do the same for me. So years later, I started smokin' me's a pipe. Smokin' a pipe relaxes me's now and brings me's closer to my daddy, who died long time ago now."

After hearing Mrs. Monroe's response to her question, Renell felt sorry that Mrs. Monroe's father had died. The thought of her own father suddenly gone from her life brought a sick feeling to the young girl's stomach. Such a thought was just too much for Renell to even consider!

Renell could now envision Mrs. Monroe as a young child taking her first puff, and Renell almost asked the older lady if she could do the same. But then one thought abruptly stopped Renell in her tracks. Renell remembered that she had heard in Sunday school that she was not supposed to defile or hurt her body by smoking tobacco and drinking alcohol. Though it was tempting, Renell knew better than to ask Mrs. Monroe, the neighborhood snitch on Oakenwaldt

Avenue, to permit Renell to smoke her pipe. Besides, she did not want Jesus to be unhappy with her.

Though she did not pose the question, Renell finally experienced momentary satisfaction as she left Mrs. Monroe's front yard that day. At least she had discovered why Mrs. Monroe smoked her pipe in the first place. Renell could not wait until she found her brother, Steven to tell him what she had just learned.

Later on, Renell pondered if Mrs. Monroe even knew that smoking was dangerous for her health and that it made Jesus sad because he made the older women's body. Renell felt sorry for Mrs. Monroe and wished she could tell her to stop smoking. But the eight-year-old knew that she did not feel comfortable telling her neighbor that. Renell realized that she now had a reason to pray for Mrs. Monroe. She did not want Mrs. Monroe to hurt or poison her body any further. In fact, as Renell thought about it, there were many people she knew who smoked. Many of her relatives saw no harm in smoking cigarettes. Renell's grandmother even sold cigarettes in her store. There were numerous commercials on television that enticed people to smoke. Renell had to admit that she herself even liked the beat of some of the songs in the cigarette television commercials.

One day, sometime later, Renell's father, Mr. Adams, overheard Renell laughing and making fun of Mrs. Monroe. He reprimanded her and told her she should not laugh at Mrs. Monroe, because the Bible states that what a person sows, he will also reap. Renell explained to her dad that she was not laughing at Mrs. Monroe, but at the words she had spoken. Renell continued, "Mrs. Monroe always says the same thing no matter how many times a day you ask her how she feels or how she is doing. All the children on Oakenwaldt Avenue can recite verbatim Mrs. Monroe's comments about how she is doing or feeling." Mr. Adams had no further response, because he knew that Renell's comments were true.

The more Renell thought about it, the more she realized that Mrs. Monroe herself actually made it difficult for anyone to be cordial to her. Now etched permanently in her young mind, Renell remembered the spanking that she and her younger brother, Steven, had received just a few weeks ago from their mother, all because of Mrs. Monroe.

The sudden punishment came without warning. It all occurred because a ball was accidentally kicked into Mrs. Monroe's yard during a kickball game that the neighborhood children were playing. However, Mrs. Monroe immediately reported to Renell and Steven's mother, Mrs. Adams, that Steven had kicked a ball into her yard and that he had then opened her gate without permission and entered her yard to get the ball back. Though the actions were not malicious, the way in which Mrs. Monroe recounted the incident to Mrs. Adams made it seem as if Renell and Steven had purposely kicked the ball into their neighbor's yard.

"To make duh matters worse," related an irate Mrs. Monroe to Mrs. Adams, "when Steven tries to gets duh ball, he steps on mys beautiful red rose bush. In his haste to gets duh ball, and leave my yard, he knocks down some of my prize dazzling flowers." Mrs. Monroe conveyed further frustration, noting that Steven knew that she was home and should have knocked on her door and simply asked for the ball. She went on to say to Mrs. Adams that she was tired of all the kids tearing up her yard. After all, she exclaimed, though many of the neighbors admittedly had beautiful flower gardens, by far, she had the prettiest flowers of anyone on Oakenwaldt Avenue.

Mrs. Monroe insisted that she would have retrieved the ball for Steven if he had only asked. Instead, she lamented her vain attempts to knock on her windowpane to get his attention fell on deaf ears, for "he paid me no mind at t'all." Mrs. Monroe stated that by the time she finally got to the front door and opened it, Steven had the ball in his hand. Mrs. Monroe concluded, "When I's askt him to give me da ball, he wouldn't do it. Insteads, he throws it o'er da fence to Renell, who catches that thar ball and runs into de house with it!"

Mrs. Adams immediately remembered Renell's quick entrance into the house. But Mrs. Adams thought it had been because her daughter had once again waited until the last minute to use the restroom. At the time of her quick entrance, Mrs. Adams had planned to tell Renell once again that she could damage her kidneys by waiting too long to use the restroom. However, before Renell had been able to exit the restroom, Mrs. Monroe's loud banging on the door had interrupted those thoughts. When Mrs. Adams went to the door and saw that it was Mrs. Monroe, she kindly opened the door and greeted her. But before she could inquire how the older lady was doing, Mrs. Monroe proceeded to recount in vivid detail the recent actions of Steven and Renell.

Mrs. Monroe ranted endlessly that none of the children on Oakenwaldt really understood the time and money it took to have and maintain a beautiful yard. After her angry tirade subsided, Mrs. Monroe told Mrs. Adams that she would appreciate it if she would make sure that Renell and Steven stayed out of her yard. She added that she thought they deserved a good old fashion spanking for being so bad.

Upon Mrs. Monroe's departure, Mrs. Adams queried Steven and Renell at length. Their mother was really interested in knowing why Steven would go into Mrs. Monroe's yard without permission. Renell and Steven knew that this was not the first time that the subject had been discussed. Mr. and Mrs. Adams wanted to keep peace in the neighborhood. Steven admitted that he just did not think about the consequences of his actions before he went into Mrs. Monroe's yard. All he had on his mind was winning the game, especially since he wanted to tag Timmy from the opposing team with the kickball before his opponent had the opportunity to make a home run. The game was tied, and all the kids were having so much fun. Steven admitted that he just totally forgot his parents' warnings and had dashed into Mrs. Monroe's yard to retrieve the wayward ball.

Renell also confessed that she had not forgotten what her parents had told her, but that she had been doggedly determined to get Steven's ball back. Why, Renell recalled, just the previous week, Mrs. Monroe warned another child whose ball had come into her yard that if the ball came into her yard again, she would keep it. Well, this wasn't just any ball, but a brand-new ball that her Auntie had just bought Steven. Renell felt it was her duty to ensure that Mrs. Monroe did not keep Steven's brand new ball! After all, what would

Mrs. Monroe do with a ball anyway? Who would want to play with Mrs. Monroe?

Because of their disobedience, Renell and Steven both received a spanking from their mother. As she punished them, Mrs. Adams reminded them of her previous instructions to stay out of Mrs. Monroe's yard. A spanking was bad enough, but that was not the end of the matter. As part of their punishment, Renell and Steven also had to remain in the house for the rest of the day. Restricted to the house on that particular day was especially painful for the two. Steven and Renell could still clearly hear the laughter and gaiety of their friends as they jovially engaged in play on the street. And to make matters worse, on the day they were punished, Renell and Steven had actually ended up on the same kickball team, which was a rare occurrence. It had happened as a result of the random pulling of names out of the hat. And to think, their team was finally winning the kick ball game!

Now, with their untimely departure from the kickball game, the rest of the kids on both teams continued the game further down Oakenwaldt Avenue. Renell knew that their friends would locate another ball. Renell's only consolation was that their team would miss her and her brother Steven, since the two of them always kicked home runs. Kickball was one of the games Renell really enjoyed playing. In fact, she had special tennis shoes she would wear just to play kickball. Now she decided to take off her shoes because she would not need them in the house.

Relegated to the house all day was the hardest part for Steven and Renell. All they could do was read books. Their mother forbade them to watch television or play with one another. Life was truly challenging that day. Though Steven's favorite show was the Adventures of Superman (he had even purchased all of Superman's comic books with his own money), he groaned and complained at the thought since he was on punishment, he would be unable to watch his next favorite family show, Leave it to Beaver.

Renell still could not grasp why Mrs. Monroe was making such a fuss over Steven retrieving the ball from her yard. Most of the neighbors had beautiful yards, adorned with a myriad of colorful flowers.

Yet no one on the whole street acted like Mrs. Monroe. Some of the neighbors would even cut their flowers and arrange them in a flower vase for display on their kitchen table, but not Mrs. Monroe.

That evening, Renell overheard her parents, Mr. and Mrs. Adams, discussing Mrs. Monroe and the incident with the kickball. Renell knew that her parents had assumed that she was asleep, but she had stirred from her previously sound slumber and was half awake as she heard her parents talk. She heard Mrs. Adams as she related the day's events to her husband, telling him how upset Mrs. Monroe was with Renell and Steven. Mr. Adams listened intently. He always felt sorry for Mrs. Monroe because she really had no friends and appeared to be very lonely since her husband had died. Of course, Renell's dad was kind and gentle to everyone he met. It was difficult for him to see anyone's faults. After his wife had spoken, however, he expressed his own annoyance at how Mrs. Monroe would daily tattle on the children as if their every little action was significant and newsworthy. After all, Mr. Adams acknowledged, Mrs. Monroe herself was once young and children would always be just that—children. Mr. Adams felt that Mrs. Monroe really needed a job to keep her busy.

In response, Mrs. Adams asserted, "She does have one, meddling with the children." They both knowingly chuckled. As they prepared for bed, Renell's father concluded, "I'll tell Steven and Renell not to go into Mrs. Monroe's yard without permission anymore, and that is all I want to hear about Mrs. Monroe. I have heard enough for a lifetime." He and his wife then broke into uncontrollable laughter as they thought about the humorous side of the whole situation. Renell began laughing herself, but her parents' jovial laughter overshadowed her own muffled giggles.

Renell felt better when she found out that Mrs. Monroe's actions also flustered her parents as well. Renell thought Mrs. Monroe had a lot of gall to come over to the Adams' home when she needed her father, Mr. Adams, to perform some task or chore for her, especially when she did not even like his children. The nerve of her, Renell indignantly noted to herself. Her father was not Mrs. Monroe's handyman! Rather than call a repairman, Mrs. Monroe always asked Mr. Adams, and he would always respond with the same polite demeanor. Maybe he should discontinue assisting her until she learned how to treat his children well, Renell mused. Of course Renell could not tell her father what she inwardly thought. He would not have stopped helping Mrs. Monroe. He was just that kind of person.

Renell told Steven that she had a secret to tell him. Since he had been asleep the night before during their parents' discussion, she couldn't wait to tell him about what she heard their parents say about Mrs. Monroe. But before she divulged her information, he had to first cross his heart and hope to die. Renell and Steven always said that to one another before they shared secrets. This was their way to ensure that they would not reveal each other's secrets.

After he had crossed his heart and hoped to die, Renell told Steven about her parents' conversation from the previous evening. Like Renell, Steven felt better too, just knowing that his parents could clearly discern Mrs. Monroe's motives. He had previously assumed his parents had been blind to the older lady's antics.

Even Mr. Eddie, the street grump, who lived across the street from the Adams family, did not act like Mrs. Monroe when the kids' kickball had rolled into his yard, and everyone knew him to be eccentric. He rarely spoke to people and then only when he felt like it. Unlike Mrs. Monroe, however, Mr. Eddie would wave to the children as they retrieved the stray ball from his yard. He loved to watch the children play ball. Some days, he would even speak to all the kids and praise them when they played a good game.

Renell surmised that the other kids must have told their parents what had happened that particular day Renell and Steven were punished. Soon afterward, many of the parents instructed their children not to play on the sidewalk in front of Mrs. Monroe's yard. Renell guessed the other parents were also tired of Mrs. Monroe's complaints about their children.

Steven and some of his friends, however, still wanted to play in their old hangout the next day after he and Renell had been punished, especially since he had concluded that the sidewalks belonged to the city rather than to Mrs. Monroe. But Steven also knew he would get in big trouble defying his parents. Renell knew her brother and was aware that he did not like to follow directions and that he really wanted to annoy Mrs. Monroe. Though their parents wished to live in peace with everyone on Oakenwaldt Avenue, the children on the street all secretly wished that Mrs. Monroe would move away since she did not like them nor did she desire harmony.

Mrs. Monroe was so mean that most of the children on Oakenwaldt Avenue literally feared her. One day, Renell overheard her aunt say to her mother, Mrs. Adams, that several of the people on Oakenwaldt Avenue were old, mean, and cantankerous. Renell made up her mind that she would look up the word cantankerous, because it was one of those words that, though she did not understand the depth of its meaning, seemed to aptly describe Mrs. Monroe. Renell really wanted to ask what the word meant, but she knew she would get in big trouble meddling in grown folks' conversation. But had she been brave enough to ask, Renell knew her aunt would have told her.

Her auntie would not bite her lips for anyone or anything. Renell loved her auntie's spunk and the fact that she would speak her mind. Her mother, on the other hand, would calmly remind Auntie that it was not always appropriate to speak her mind. Mrs. Adams would wisely say, "Keep people thinking about what you are thinking, don't tell them everything. Smile and look at them and keep moving on." But Renell noticed that following that wise advice was especially hard for Auntie who wanted to get things off her chest.

While Mrs. Monroe lived on the left of the Adams family, the Jones family lived on their right. Mr. Jones was a minister, but even at her young age, Renell noticed that he had some characteristics not typically associated with ministry. For instance, residents knew him to be stingy, selfish, a wifebeater, and a busybody. Though he had several children himself, most residents on Oakenwaldt Avenue assumed he did not like children either. Though he was not quite as bad as Mrs. Monroe, he was not much better.

The children on Oakenwaldt Avenue knew that the most beautiful, juicy green apples grew on the apple tree located in Mr. Jones's front yard. The tree was located next to the fence that divided the Adams property from the Jones property. In September and October of each year, the delicious, ripe apples would fall almost daily in both yards. Mr. Jones sternly reminded the Adams' children and all the children on Oakenwaldt Avenue that they could not have the apples that fell. It didn't matter if they landed on the Adams' yard because they came from his tree. Renell knew Steven would pick up the apples and save them to eat later.

A majority of the children were afraid of Mr. Jones every day, except on Sundays. Renell did not quite understand it, but for some reason, he was a friendly person on Sundays. Mrs. Jones, his wife, was the antithesis of Mr. Jones. She was always a very humble and sweet lady. When he was not at their home, she would observe the children outside playing, and she would lean out through the screen door on their front porch and tell the children that they could help themselves to the apples.

Renell often wondered why her family had such mean people living on both sides of them. And yet, there was a bright spot! The Rawls family lived two houses from Renell on the right side of the Jones family. Mr. and Mrs. Rawls had two daughters, Cindy and Ginny, who were older than Renell, but she had fun playing games such as jacks and blind man's bluff with the two girls. The Rawls and Adams families were close friends, and they often participated in many family activities together. Mr. Rawls worked at the Mansfield Tire Company, while Mrs. Rawls was a homemaker like Renell's mother, Mrs. Adams. Mrs. Rawls and Mrs. Adams often enjoyed exchanging recipes.

5

Liberty Park

Oakenwaldt Avenue was only one of the many streets that comprised Renell's community. At least, Grace Street was a much easier street to pronounce and was in close proximity to Oakenwaldt Avenue. Because it contained so many noteworthy landmarks, Grace Street was a popular, well-known street in Mansfield, Ohio. For instance, St. Mary's Catholic Church and Liberty Park were both located on Grace Street.

Liberty Park was a well-known park in town, and Renell always thoroughly enjoyed her visits there. At Liberty Park, there were a variety of activities for her entire family to enjoy on any spring or summer day, including a swimming pool, the baseball diamond, the spacious picnic area dotted with picnic tables, the tennis courts, the numerous swing sets and the high sliding board, from which Renell and her friends could launch, clad in their swim suits, directly into the large pond located at the front entrance to the park. Additionally, Renell delighted in the park's picturesque pond, home to several birds, ducks and geese.

In the winter, when the temperature would plunge below thirty-two degrees, the pond would become one of Mansfield's most popular ice-skating rinks and a magnetic attraction and meeting place for locals. However, Renell and the other neighborhood children knew that it was unlawful and forbidden to even think of skating on the frozen pond before the city's recreation department had inspected the ice to ensure it was safe for the young, eager ice-skaters. Once, Renell recalled sadly, there had been an accident at the pond when a few kids began to ice-skate on the ice before the ice had been inspected and the children lost their lives. The still recent, heart wrenching, tragedy served as a poignant reminder to the children on Oakenwaldt Avenue to carefully follow safety precautions and guidelines.

During the times she visited Liberty Park, Renell loved to watch everyone ice skate on the pond. While on the ice, parents often had their toddlers and little children in tow, held closely by their sides. Renell found it fun to observe the tiny, faltering timid steps, the unavoidable bumps and the repeated falls of the youngsters as they struggled to learn to stand erect and move gracefully on the frozen ice.

Though Renell loved Liberty Park, she never wanted to go ice-skating because she could not tolerate the often-frigid temperatures for long periods of time. To Renell, the cold, icy weather and frigid temperatures seemed to penetrate through her to the very core of her being, which would leave her feeling miserable! Despite this, however, Renell always remained enthralled by the beautiful white snow and its glistening brilliance in the sun as she viewed the winter wonderland from any one of the several windows in her family's home.

Despite Renell's seeming aversion to the frigid temperatures, she would endure sled rides in the bitter cold in twenty-minute increments, but not a minute longer. On the other hand, Renell's brothers, if allowed to, had no aversion to the subzero temperatures and would often play on their sleds in the snow for hours.

Although she was not an avid ice skater, Renell enjoyed roller-skating immensely and could spend endless hours in the spring and summer weather perfecting her natural skill and ability in the sport. In fact, Renell first learned to roller-skate on Oakenwaldt Avenue with the other children. She and her friends would skate up and down the street for hours. Soon, they learned to race one another. It was an activity that the adults liked to watch the children do as well.

On Monday evenings, Renell, along with her family and friends, would go roller-skating at North Lake Skating Rink. The skating rink was always a hubbub of activity as people regularly mingled, visited and had fun. In addition, curious bystanders, onlookers and the gathering crowds were freely entertained as they watched roller-skating at its best. Even at eight years old, Renell was a gifted skater who, with adeptness and agility, could skate forward and backward at high speeds. Renell eagerly anticipated every Monday, especially in the summers, because she could participate in the weekly Monday-night skating at the rink.

6

Spring of 1958

Since the first grade, Renell had always awaited the arrival of each spring with joyous anticipation! However, the spring of 1958 held extra special significance for the lively eight-year-old. As always, with every spring's arrival, there were countless, fun-filled events scheduled at school, in the neighborhood, and at church. The spring carnival at Liberty Park, sponsored by the school, was full of events and mouthwatering foods. In addition, the sixth grade concert, spearheaded every spring by the sixth grade teachers, always featured an array of festive activities, including a special soloist from Oakenwaldt Avenue. Several memorable birthday parties and a spectacular end-of-the-school-year celebration held in early June topped every fun-filled season.

Renell especially loved that daylight savings time began on April 27, 1958, which meant the kids would have more time outside to play before dinner and before the streetlights came on. As the early spring season slowly emerged from the arms of a snowy, cold winter, all the children would, as if on cue, finish their homework and quickly scurry outside to play together before dinner. While Renell and her friends had their nonstop jacks competition on the sidewalk, further down the street, others were absorbed in their own hopscotch tournament. Renell, however, especially loved playing jacks with her girlfriends and her siblings. To play jacks successfully, Renell and her friends had to be very coordinated and be able to do several things at once. First they had to scatter the jacks onto the playing surface. Then they would toss the ball into the air, and finally they would pick up the jacks and the ball. Renell considered herself a master at the game!

As with most other spring seasons, the spring of 1958 was no different, as Renell and Sherry helped Mrs. Adams, Mrs. Grant, and Renell's Auntie plant various kinds of flower bulbs around each of their homes. The girls thought, *It's great fun to plant the bulbs.* With eager anticipation, they would anxiously await the blooming of the beautiful plants, which invariably occurred during the early summer months.

Of all the ladies, Mrs. Adams had what people called a green thumb. She had several different kinds of gorgeous perennials. They ranged from daylilies, daffodils, and tulips, which would bloom each year without fail and majestically clothe the family's backyard with an array of brilliant colors.

The flowers Mrs. Adams planted years ago in the front and along the left side of the house were slowly blooming. To Renell and her friends, the flowers made an exquisite bouquet as they gracefully encircled a portion of the Adams' home. Renell could never forget the names of some of the beautiful flowers such as the gorgeous crocuses, dahlias, gladioli, and the climbing red rose bushes. When people strolled past the Adams' home or visited the family, they would invariably admire the beautiful array of flowers that surrounded the house. The inviting aroma of the flowers lingered in the air as passersby continued to walk past the house.

Easter was always a fun time, but that year, it was especially memorable for Renell and the other children on Oakenwaldt Avenue. The last day of class was on Thursday, and they would not have to return to school until the following Tuesday! While the Adams family consistently attended church services every Wednesday and Friday nights throughout the year, night service on Good Friday was particularly significant. It was during Good Friday night services that the church also held feet washing and communion.

Renell vividly recalled during Good Friday night service, her mother was especially touched by the Lord in such a magnificent way. For Renell, it was as if an actual veil of glory—the invisible, intangible aura of the Almighty God of the Bible—surrounded Mrs. Adams. Regarding her life-changing experience, Mrs. Adams herself exultantly proclaimed, "The Lord's presence lifted a heavy burden that I had been carrying since Donald passed!"

Renell did not understand what her mother meant by that remark. However, as Mrs. Adams uttered those words, her young eight-year-old daughter witnessed a sudden transformation as a broad smile and joy-filled countenance replaced the previously stoic facial expression Mrs. Adams had worn like a mask since the death of Renell's brother. Without a doubt, Renell's mother had remained kind and caring through the loss of Donald, but her once-contagious smile and laughter had been visibly absent since the passing of her son.

Despite being wise for her age, Renell could not grasp the pain, agony, and indescribable grief that her parents, older siblings, family members, and close family friends had experienced with the passing of Renell's older brother. Though only eight years old, she remembered her brother who embodied such warmth, laughter, compassion, and love. Since his passing, the house was no longer the same, his absence so keenly felt with each passing day. What a blessed power of healing was vividly displayed to the entire family during that powerful Good Friday service.

Unquestionably, Easter represented a joyous event anticipated by Renell and all the children on Oakenwaldt Avenue. The young girls donned in their new Easter bonnets and pretty pastel dresses and coats and the young boys in their new suits, new shirts, ties and creased pants would proudly parade their recently purchased attire during the Sunday school and church services. Of course, Easter was not Easter without the traditional Easter speeches, church plays and programs that depicted the resurrection, and the Easter baskets full of candies and other delectable delights each child received.

The traditional Easter program at Renell's church was held during Sunday school. Without fail, the subsequent Easter morning church service was so touching that Renell, immersed in the annual dramatization, always felt she too was one of those who had sighted Jesus after his resurrection. After the church service, the Adams family gathered with other family members for a traditional, old-fashioned Easter dinner at the home of Renell's grandmother. Gaiety and laughter soon filled every corner of the modest home as aunts, uncles, cousins, parents, and siblings came together to celebrate the joyous occasion, complete with tantalizing, mouthwatering dishes, fun, and laughter.

Renell's grandmother was an accomplished cook and the food was both delicious and exquisite! Every year, Renell's grandmother lovingly and with meticulous care cooked each dish with her family members in mind. Though Renell's mother's face still reflected a radiant glow, Renell noticed that her mother did not seem to exhibit her usual level of energy. Maybe Mrs. Adams was tired because so much was going on in preparing for the Easter program.

With the Easter vacation behind them, all the children on Oakenwaldt Avenue, as if in blind unison, began counting down the remaining days of the school year. With unbridled anticipation, Renell and her friends could hardly wait for all that summer would bring, such as sleeping late, long, fun-filled days of play out of doors and enjoying the hot, leisurely days of a much needed, long awaited summer vacation.

Meanwhile, Renell's brothers and other teenagers on the street were eagerly awaiting the Mansfield Mehock Relays. The Mehock Relays were an annual competitive regional track-and-field meet held every April in Mansfield. The competition was open to any high school student who was a winner in their school in any given track and field events who hailed from Ohio, Michigan Indiana, and Ontario, Canada. Many of the families on Oakenwaldt Avenue enjoyed attending the annual event. It provided the opportunity for everyone to encourage and cheer on friends and family members who were chosen to participate.

Without fail, the smell of mouthwatering snacks from the food booths during the Mansfield Mehock Relays would quickly fill the air and entice unsuspecting passersby to stop and buy the delicious hotdogs, popcorn and other food items. That particularly warm and pleasant weekend, Renell thoroughly enjoyed the Mansfield Mehock Relays. Surprisingly, it was warm and pleasant which was a huge blessing as Mansfield typically had an extensive history of snow days in April.

On most Saturday afternoons, Renell enjoyed going over to her grandmother's house to work in her store. Her grandmother was her mother's mother, and she was called Mama Jones by her grandchildren. The store was located in the front of her grandmother's home where she resided and typically referred to as the neighborhood or Lily Street corner store. Renell loved Mama Jones's store because it sold all the snacks that she loved such as sodas (Pepsi, root beer, orange, cherry), Jones Potato Chips, and candy. Renell's grandmother also sold cigarettes to adults. Renell enjoyed stocking the shelves of the store and eating her share of chips. She did not receive payment for her services because, according to her grandmother, she ate up all of her pay!

In addition to eating the scrumptious snacks while working, Renell enjoyed socializing with the customers when they visited the store. Often, Renell's grandmother would remind her that she was supposed to be working and the store patrons should not just hang out in the store unless they were going to purchase products. Renell did not quite understand, but she obeyed her grandmother and dutifully returned her focus to her work. During the summer months, Renell would leave the store at approximately seven o'clock on Saturday evenings so she could prepare for Sunday school and church the next day, her stomach filled with chips and Pepsi. During their summer break, Renell and several of her cousins would spend much of their time with their grandmother on Lily Street.

Mama Jones had a shiny black-and-yellow Buick that she drove all over town. Renell enjoyed those times when her grandmother would pick her up after school. Her grandmother was an avid sports fan. She loved the Cleveland Indians baseball team. Each time she attended the games in Cleveland, she would take a few of her grandchildren with her. The grandkids would enjoy the peanuts, popcorn, and hotdogs she would buy them. When she did not attend the ball games in person, Mama Jones would simultaneously listen to the games on her radio while she also watched the same game on television. When asked why she did both, Renell's grandmother would always remark, "I want to see and hear everything going on." That was puzzling to Renell because the television also had a sports commentator who provided a vivid account of every play that occurred during the game.

Mama Jones kept herself busy doing something all day. She was always sewing or making quilts for the family. Clothes that were too small for the family were given to her and they soon became part of the quilt she was making. Renell thought it was easier to just go to JCPenney or Sears and Roebuck and purchase blankets. It took her grandmother lots of time and patience to make the quilts, but she loved what she was doing. Mama Jones would knowingly remark, "Quilts are a conversation piece, and they tell a story. One day you will remember when it is on your bed, the time and effort I took to make sure you were warm."

The spring of 1958 was quickly passing, and summer was fast approaching. Renell was exuberant that the summer season was almost upon them. She anxiously anticipated wearing tennis shoes and sandals each day (except, of course, Sunday). And now, with every weekend, not only did the ice cream trucks begin to travel the well-worn route through Oakenwaldt Avenue and other streets in the community, but the Dairy Queen, which was closed during the winter months had now reopened for business. As if it had happened overnight, brilliant, green leaves seemed to once again fill the naked trees previously left bare after the cold, icy winter. Renell now awakened each morning to the joyous chorus of birds chirping loudly, as if in response to the unspoken proclamation that winter was over and summer, imminent. Flies and other flying insects invade picnics, cookouts and other public gatherings the family attended. But Renell did not mind—summer was almost here!

The last week of school was like a whirlwind. Everything was discombobulated! Children were turning in their library books, paying fines for missing or lost books, cleaning out their desks, and checking the lost and found for jackets, sweaters, and other valuables that belonged to them. The sixth grade classes had a party in the cafeteria, and the long-awaited award ceremony was held in the gymnasium for the entire student body. Lunches were served without posted menus and some of the children seemed to repeatedly get in trouble. The students knew their grade cards were complete and ready for distribution and now all the teachers had to write on the cards were absences and days present. Recess was longer and different classes had kickball tournaments. Those tournaments were the best time because even if students were not playing, at least the class could sit on the grass and watch and cheer for the games. No one wanted to stay in the school building. All the action was outside on the field!

Finally, the last day of school, which was a half day, arrived! Students brought packed lunches from home and watched movies shown on a 16 mm projector as they anxiously waited to see if they had passed to the next grade. The students in Renell's class exchanged telephone numbers and each promised to call one another at least once during the summer. Renell knew she would see some of her classmates at Liberty Park's swimming pool or on the side of the park that held the swings and jungle gyms. Others would go to Liberty Park for their softball games and tennis matches. After all, there were numerous activities always going on for the entire family.

The anticipated moment of receiving the final report card came. It was as if all the teachers passed out the reports to the students in unison. Cheers could be heard throughout the entire school, and then the bell rung! Some students were crying and saying they would miss coming to school. Renell had enough friends on Oakenwaldt to play with and she could see the school building, which was down the street. She felt sorry for those who were crying because she sensed they must not have many friends to play with. Those children just needed to live on Oakenwaldt, Renell surmised, where there were plenty of children and lots of activities going on.

Summer vacation was a reality! Students were running out of the school building, loudly shouting and sharing with anyone who would listen, "I passed!" Renell knew there would be celebrations up and down Oakenwaldt Avenue. She was ready for the fun to begin!

The first week of summer vacation was relaxing and quiet on Oakenwaldt. Renell did not realize just how much she would enjoy sleeping later in the morning. The only day she had during the school year to sleep later was on Saturday.

Although it was summer vacation and she knew her mother would give the children time to sleep in, Renell also knew that morning devotions were set in stone in the Adams family. One of the scriptures her mother would quote daily was found in Proverbs 3:6: "In all thy ways acknowledge Him and He shall direct your paths." Renell's mother would share with her children that this verse meant that Jesus wanted Renell and her sister and brothers to trust the Lord and to know that he was always there with them and if they would listen, he would always direct them in truth. As a result, Renell would feel a sense of fear when she was not obedient. She would say, "Lord, please forgive me, I know I was wrong in what my decisions were." Renell thought the Lord was telling her mother when she disobedient, because her mother always found out.

Each day after morning devotions, consumption of breakfast, completion of morning chores and reading time, Renell could go outside and play until lunchtime. Mrs. Adams was a firm believer that her children should take a nap after lunch. Renell didn't mind lying down for the nap, but she knew she would miss some of the action during the nap time. After the rest time, Renell was glad to be back outside with her friends until dinnertime.

One of her chores each evening was setting the dinner table for the family dinner. She would diligently run home, wash her hands, and set the table. Renell could hardly wait to eat the scrumptious food. The delicious aromas of Mrs. Adams' cooking had already slowly drifted through the evening air outside and had warmly greeted her as she walked up the entrance to the family home.

All the family would eat dinner together and talk about their day. Mr. Adams always said the grace. Each child would then recite their Bible verse. Renell enjoyed setting the table because she could pick out the tablecloth and napkins to put on the table. Mrs. Adams had sewn many beautiful different kinds and colors of tablecloths and napkins. The ones used on Sunday had pretty lace sewn all around the edges.

Renell's mother also made tablecloths for her young daughter's little table located on the front porch, alongside Renell's other toys and doll babies. Renell would only put her tablecloth on her table when she and her friends played house and tea was served. Her auntie had bought her a tea set. Renell enjoyed entertaining her friends, but, instead of serving tea, Renell and her friends would drink juice or Kool-Aid in the little teacups and saucers.

After Renell and her friends drank their tea, Mrs. Adams would assist the girls in washing up the dishes. The dishes would then go back in Renell's basket until she would use them again. Mrs. Adams always told her to clean up once she finished playing with something while her friends were there because if she did not do that, she would have to clean up everything alone. She learned her lesson! One afternoon, her friends left abruptly and everything was a mess. Renell thought her mom was going to help her, but she did not. Renell cried and cried, but no one would help her. She cleaned up the play area on the porch by herself, and that never happened again!

A big *no* in the Adams house was going into the refrigerator before you washed your hands. You would get punished for that, and that was a rule all the Adams children followed. Her mother knew their hands were not clean from being outside or just being in the house touching things. Renell wondered if the milkman washed his hands before placing the milk in the refrigerator, but Renell decided she would just ponder the answer to that question in her mind.

Many days, the young girls on Oakenwaldt Avenue would play school or house with their dolls on the Adams' front porch. Each girl would take turns being the teacher. Renell had a chalkboard and they all enjoyed writing notes on the board. There was never a dull moment playing school and imitating their teachers. The boys would not usually play school or house, but they enjoyed playing cowboys and Indians and rolling tires up and down the street. Many of the boys would try to get inside the tire and roll down the street. When getting inside the tire, their thoughts never seemed to dwell on the possible danger involved.

Most of the families had swing sets in the backyard with a sliding board. At the bottom of the Adams' sliding board was a small pile of dirt. The pile of dirt would turn to a mud puddle when it would rain outside. After the rain, the children had tons of fun sliding down the slide and jumping over the mud puddle. Many times they would get their tennis shoes muddy from all the fun.

Renell also enjoyed playing with the boys as well. She really enjoyed climbing the two big trees in her backyard. One was a weeping willow tree, and the other was a pear tree, which had a grape vine growing almost to the top of it. Several grape vines had grown below the tree and had developed into a little grape orchard. The most delicious, sweet, purple grapes were picked from those vines.

Renell could hardly wait for those grapes to ripen each summer. Some grapes would ripen before the others. Mrs. Adams and the other mothers would make grape jelly to be spread on biscuits, rolls or on mouth-watering peanut butter sandwiches. Mrs. Adams learned from her mother how to can jelly. The orchard each summer produced enough grapes for Renell's mother to can jelly to last the family the entire winter. Renell enjoyed watching her mother make the jelly. Once her mom had finished, she filled the jelly in mason pint jars and sealed them with a tight lid. The jelly was stored in the cabinet, to be eaten throughout the winter. Yummy!

The flowers were blooming up and down the street. Oakenwaldters took pride in keeping their yards neat. The boys were taught how to mow the yard with the push mowers. Mowing the lawns seemed like an easy task when their fathers did it, but the job was not completed until the lawn was raked from the cut grass. It was an all-day job when the mowing was assigned to the young men. They took so many breaks and complained that they were tired and that it was so difficult pushing the lawn mowers. They took Kool-Aid breaks, water breaks and lunch breaks, but they knew the job had to be completed before their fathers came home from work. The young men made sure, however, that the complaining only took place among themselves and never to their fathers.

Mr. Adams would tell his sons they were in training because one day they would have their own home and they would know how to do necessary things around the house. Renell thought that would be a very long time and that they would really get a lot of practice before then. Each week, the lawn had to be mowed. Renell wanted to learn how to do that as well. It really looked cool and she was intrigued how the reel of blades revolved around as the lawn mower was pushed. The grass blades extended between the cutting blades and a bed knife, which worked much like scissors or shears to cut the grass. Occasionally, one of Renell's brothers would let her push the lawn mower. She soon learned it was not an easy job and she started getting water when they mowed the lawn. On mowing day, Renell was suddenly glad that she was a girl!

7

Summer Fun

Though July swiftly made a hot and muggy entrance, the Fourth of July was a blast for the Adams family. They had a big family picnic with their uncles, aunts, cousins and others who gathered on the Company Line. So much food was prepared for the picnic. Just name it and it was probably there! Renell loved hotdogs on the grill and she was allowed to eat all her heart desired on the Fourth of July. After it turned dark, the entire family enjoyed the fireworks that lit up the balmy Ohio sky. The children especially enjoyed the booming, buzzing, hissing and crackling noise the fireworks made.

The following day was Renell's time to go to her grandmother's and work in the store. She was excited and anticipated spending time with cousins who would also be staying with their grandmother. They already knew that they would be pulling weeds out of the flower garden, filling up the coolers with different drinks and sweeping the sidewalk daily. Her grandmother had plenty of chores for them to do.

Mama Jones loved flowers and Renell soon figured out why her mother also loved them as well. As a child, Mrs. Adams had helped her mom maintain a beautiful flower garden. She was taught how to fertilize the soil, plant the flowers in the soil and the correct way to water the flowers. Once the flowers were planted, their healthy growth required additional attention, so Mrs. Adams periodically pulled the weeds that grew in the garden. Renell and her cousins would plant the annuals in gorgeous pots that Mama Jones hand painted. They learned how to put rocks in the bottom of the pots, to mix the soil and fertilizer together, to placed them next in the pots and, finally, to place the flowers deep in the soil. The end results were beautiful flowerpots on proud display around the front of Mama Jones' house and in her store. Renell's grandmother's favorite saying as they were planting was "Give me my flowers while I live so I can enjoy their beauty and enjoy the different smells." Renell observed that her grandmother got her wish because she certainly had plenty of flowers to enjoy in her home and yard.

For Renell, the reward for a good day's work was the delicious, delectable aromas that came from her grandmother's kitchen. Mama Jones enjoyed cooking and making sure that the children were well fed and full. Also they were allowed to have a Pepsi or another drink of their choice with their dinner. The word would spread fast that Renell and her cousins were working in the store. Many of the children would come by and buy candy and talk to Renell and her cousins. Each evening they would play in front of the house with some of the children on Lily Street.

Renell did not miss Oakenwaldt because she enjoyed being with her cousins and the children on Lily Street. She also knew her grandmother enjoyed having company, and she always cooked their favorite foods. Delicious fried chicken, fried pork chops, rice pudding, homemade yeast biscuits, and some kind of green vegetables were some of Renell's requests for one of the evening meals. Her grandmother had the best syrup for the biscuits, which was called Alaga. Alaga was so delicious that her brother, Eugene, would make syrup sandwiches. Mama Jones would also prepare a big breakfast each morning and if they had leftover biscuits, instead of syrup, they would spread homemade jelly on them. Along with their breakfast Mama Jones would give them a cup of coffee if you would call it that. It was really more milk and sugar then coffee. Renell and her cousins would feel grown up sipping on coffee with their grandmother.

Each evening, Renell would call home to find out how her family was doing. Mama Jones mentioned to Renell that the young girl's mother had not been feeling well and that she needed to go to the doctor. Specifically, Mama Jones wanted her daughter to find out what was causing the persistent, chronic dry cough she was experiencing and why she continued to feel so tired. When an increasing look of concern and worry began to develop on Renell's face, her grandmother would reassure her that her mom would be fine. But Renell didn't know what to believe. After all, she had heard the same words of consolation regarding her brother Donald. It turned out he was not alright and he was no longer with them. Sensing Renell's distress, her grandmother quickly got Renell's mind on other things when she told the eight-year-old that they were going to eat some ice cream, watch *The Real McCoys* and enjoy one another.

Her grandmother was a stewardess at Mitchell Chapel AME Church, and the stewardesses were assigned reserved seats. When Renell sat with her grandmother in church, she felt special. In just two days, it would be Sunday and Renell would go to church with her grand-mother and her cousins. Stewardesses were women appointed by the pastor to serve as special assistant to the stewards. Their responsi-bilities included preparing the physical arrangements for the pulpit, prepare the elements for Lord's Supper, and Holy Baptism, and many other duties.

Renell admitted that the length of the Sunday services at Mama Jones' church compared to the length of the Sunday services at Renell's family's church were unequaled. When she attended church services with Mama Jones, the church services would conclude by twelve noon, while at the Adams' church, the congregants would still be singing and enjoying the Lord. At Renell's family's church, there was no established length of the service or specified time to conclude. Time was not an issue when the Adams were in the presence of the Lord. On the other hand, Mama Jones would note the difference in time. However, when she attended worship services at the Adams' church, she enjoyed the soul-stirring music.

Each Sunday, you could always go by and eat a mouthwatering meal at Mama Jones. She always cooked enough for those family members who would stop by to see her. Just as she did with her own mother, Renell could smell the aroma permeating the air from Mama Jones' delicious fried chicken, fried corn, turnip or mustard green and her mouth-watering, hot, buttery biscuits, topped off by her grandmother's cake and ice cream for dessert.

Renell loved and enjoyed Sunday school. She was familiar with the lessons from morning devotions and she would answer the questions that her teacher asked without hesitation. Sister Wallace, the nursery and beginners' teacher, taught many of her lessons through songs. Renell and the students would clap their hands and jump and down, often responding to the catchy beat and rhythm of the songs. Sister Wallace taught the class the "Books of the Bible" song. Renell learned all the sixty-six books before turning six years old.

Dinnertime after church on Sunday at the Adams' house was the time each family member shared what was taught in their individual Sunday school class. Mrs. Adams always reminded them to not just be a hearer of the rich word of God, but to be a doer.

Renell enjoyed the young people's meeting, which met the first Sunday of each month at six o'clock. The young people's president had fun, exciting, and innovative programs planned for each meeting. Trivia Bible games were the hit at any of the meetings. The Trivia Bible game and Bible Sword Drill were both intriguing and competitive and Renell always enjoyed them. The Bible Sword Drill was a team game in which everyone's Bible knowledge was on display. The sword was the Bible, which the participant used to locate the book of the Bible, the chapter and the verse given to the group by the youth leader. Renell thought it was an exciting way to learn the books of the Bible. At the start of each game, all Bibles were closed as the participant awaited instructions. The leader would hold up the Bible and say, "Swords ready!" and would say the book, chapter, and verse. Everyone would repeat the book, chapter, and verse that was given. Next the leader would say "ready" and all participants would hold up their Bible. Finally the leader would say loudly "go" and the race would begin. It was so exciting to hear and see the pages of the Bible flip as, in eager anticipation, each participant excitedly attempted to locate the correct scripture. The person who found the verse would stand and read that particular verse and would receive a point if the correct scripture had been read. The participant with the most points won. To Renell, the young people's meeting was much more exciting and enjoyable than the Wednesday and Friday night services.

Wednesday night always began with prayer, a song, and finally the Bible class. Before the lesson was taught, Bishop Chester always asked, "Are there any questions that anyone might have from your personal Bible study time, devotions or family discussion? Each member should have a daily designated bible time as well as family devotion time. Just as one eats natural food, the soul should also be fed spiritual food, which is the Word of God. The Bible should be more than a book displayed on the coffee table keeping records of births, deaths, marriages and other important events in the family." Bishop Chester then taught the weekly lesson after the questions were answered. Renell learned that each lesson provided spiritual and practical guidance for everyday living and served as a tool for witnessing and drawing others to the kingdom.

Friday night service was filled with prayer, soul-stirring singing, testimonies and preaching. Testimonies were shared to witness to others about the power, miracles and faithfulness of the Lord in their life. Some church members testified about healing they received in their bodies, protection from accidents, salvation, having food, shelter, clothing, how the Lord showed up in dire circumstances, answered prayers, provided deliverance, opened doors that the enemy had closed and closed doors that the enemy had opened. The saints would always acknowledge the Lord, praise him and give him thanks. Some of the testimonies would make Renell smile or cry and others would really make her think about how grateful she was to know the Lord and all the promises in the Word that were available to her, if she were obedient and had faith. Renell and the other saints would feel a sense of awe as they heard the miracles that occurred and the power of trusting in the Lord! As Renell's mother wisely reminded her, "Testimonies were given to build up your faith in the Lord and know the power of his Word." Renell enjoyed hearing some of the older saints say the same identical testimony each week. Most of the children could recite them verbatim.

Every year in July, the Westinghouse factory would shut down its plant for two weeks. When it did so, Mr. Adams would also take the same two weeks off from his business for the family's vacation. The family would go to Alabama to visit Mr. Adams's parents and to Detroit to visit other family members. Renell remembers vividly traveling to Alabama late one night.

Everyone was asleep in the car when Mr. Adams stopped at a gasoline station in Kentucky to get fuel. When Renell awakened, she had to use the restroom. Spotting the ladies restroom, she quickly exited the car. As she was quickly running toward the restroom, she heard her father cry out, "Renell, stop, baby, where are you going?" Renell replied, "Daddy, I have to go to the bathroom and I see the sign." Mr. Adams then explained to his young eight year old daughter that she could not go into the restroom because it was for "white people only." Renell really did not understand that and told him that she really had to use the bathroom. So her father took her behind the building to the restroom marked "Colored Bathroom." Renell went into a facility that was nasty, unkempt and that smelled of urine and other foul, disgusting odors.

When she came out, there were tears in her father's eyes. He explained to her about segregation and why they usually left home at midnight. He stated, "The South was so prejudiced when he was a child and I wanted to get out of there as soon as I graduated from high school." He did exactly that at the age of sixteen. He went on to tell Renell why they always prepared and brought their own food, especially fried chicken, in the car as they traveled and why they traveled in the middle of the night. Mr. Adams said, "We could not buy food inside the restaurant, but we could go to a back window and order food. I refused to be belittled! We always left when we knew all of you children would sleep through the night. You would be the one to wake up." Renell did not understand all she was told, but she was glad that she lived in Mansfield, Ohio, and that she could go to the restroom if she saw a sign that said "Ladies' Restroom."

After their vacation, there was just a little over a month left of summer fun. The Sunday school picnic was something to look forward to in August, along with several other outings. Renell knew that every Friday and Saturday evening she would smell the mouthwatering ribs from Mr. Jones' barbeque pit. He was ready for the customers to come and purchase their weekend dinners.

During the summer months on Oakenwaldt Avenue, the boys continued to play basketball games down at the school's basketball court during the day and, in the evenings, the younger children played hide-and-seek near their homes. The street light next to Mrs. Monroe's house served as the base that each player had to touch to avoid getting tagged and eliminated from the game. As the summer nights passed, the evenings began to get a little chilly. Labor Day was fast approaching and the first day of school for Renell and all of her friends would begin the day after. The week before Labor Day, the teachers came back to school to set up their rooms. If teachers spotted children on the playground playing, they would go outside and ask for help in moving boxes, setting up the classroom, washing the blackboards, and assisting in other errands for them. Some of the teachers would give the children money or other treats for their assistance.

Parents were reading and scanning the papers for sales on school clothes, shoes, and supplies. JCPenney, Montgomery Wards, and Sears and Roebuck were competing for business. Renell knew that the time was drawing near to stop wearing tennis shoes each day. She could wear her tennis shoes after school until it snowed and then no more tennis shoes until the following spring. She had flat, narrow feet and Renell's mom acknowledged that Renell's shoes were very expensive. She needed three pairs of shoes—two were for school and a black patent leather pair for church. The gym floor was always cleaned and waxed over the summer, and the students were to only wear tennis shoes if they were participating in an indoor sport on the school gym floor.

It was fun going shoe shopping with her mom. Siblings felt the same way when it was their time. On yet another day, Renell and her mother would shop for skirts and blouses for school. Auntie would buy Renell beautiful dresses for church and that would mark yet another day that all the attention was on her. Yes, just her and Auntie. Auntie would also buy Renell cancan slips to go under her dresses to make them stand out. Mama Jones would make Renell some skirts and dresses for school as well. Indeed, Renell was thankful for her clothes. She carefully hung them up in her closet and gazed longingly at each outfit, eagerly awaiting the approaching days when she would wear them. Renell was ready for the first, second, and all the days of the first week of school.

Renell and her friends on Oakenwaldt knew school would start in a week, and they decided to sleep a little later in the mornings and come outside later in the afternoon to socialize. Renell wrote letters to her older brother Lewis who was in college, telling him all the happenings around the house and the people of Oakenwaldt. She wanted him to get a letter from her, and in return, he would write her back.

Renell talked to Lewis every week when he called to speak with the family and to check in. He enjoyed meeting new friends and enjoyed his close proximity to relatives in Dayton who would pick him up on weekends to spend that time with them. Renell's parents felt so much better knowing someone nearby was there for him. He attended Central State College in Wilberforce, Ohio. Renell knew that her sister would also attend that same college as soon as she graduated. Renell knew Lewis would look after their sister to make sure that she adjusted to college life, the city, and being away from home. Yvonne would be attending a church in Xenia on Sunday. The church was part of the organization that the Adams' family fellowship also attended in Mansfield. Yvonne knew several of the young adults from the church camp in Zanesville that she had attended for many summers and she was also a counselor there. Yvonne would see some of the young people at the church in Xenia, Ohio, each Sunday. Church was number one in Yvonne's heart. She loved the Lord and all church services.

Yes, Renell was excited. A new school year was just around the corner! And Renell and everyone she knew, were ready for all that the autumn would bring.

Disappointment, Devastation and Hope for Tomorrow

Labor Day was a fun and relaxing day for the families on Oakenwaldt. Most of the factories and businesses were closed to observe the holiday. Many of the families cooked their lunch and dinner out on their grills. The aroma of food cooking on the grills slowly floating through the air only added to the warmth and charm of the busy street.

When the children gathered on Oakenwaldt Avenue after lunch that afternoon, each one shared their own expectations of how they felt the first day of class would be. They discussed what they would wear and determined what time to meet to walk together to school. Earlier than usual, the street soon emptied as Renell and all her friends left that afternoon to take their baths and retire to bed early. The first day of school was the next day and they had to be ready! Renell read a chapter from one of the Boxcar Children's books, said her prayers and tried to go to sleep. But she had a hard time falling asleep. Her one prayer for the first day of school was to ask the Lord for the teacher of her choice.

Tuesday morning, the family was up early eating, having their family devotions, and waiting to leave the house for school. Renell kissed her mom and ran outside to meet her friends to walk down the street. Everyone looked so groomed—new clothes, shoes, fresh haircuts, and hairstyles. They knew the first day routine. Everyone would go to the front of the school, get in line according to grade level, and wait until they heard their name called by the teacher they were assigned to for the year. Parents were waiting as well in the line.

Tuesday morning, the children in the Adams family arose early to eat, have family devotions, dress and wait to leave the house for school. Renell kissed her mom and ran outside to meet her friends to walk down the street. Renell and her friends looked impeccable and spotless—new clothes, new shoes, fresh haircuts and hairstyles. Aware of the first day of school routine, everyone would go to the front of the school, get in line according to grade level and wait until they heard their name called by the teacher they were assigned to for the year. Some parents were waiting in the line with their children as well.

Renell looked around and glimpsed her mother standing with her brother in the second grade line. Mrs. Adams was going to make sure Steven got to the right class and she also wanted to meet his teacher. She would then meet Renell's teacher after school. Renell waved to her mother and brother.

After Steven went into the school building with his teacher and his new classmates, Mrs. Adams proceeded to the third-grade line to find out the name of Renell's teacher. Mrs. Adams so hoped that Renell got the teacher she wanted! But when Renell did not get the teacher she wanted, Renell's mother immediately detected the pain in her young daughter's eyes and quickly assured Renell that it was still going to be a great year. Renell felt like crying and turning around and going back home with her mother, never to return to school for the entire year!

Renell's third grade teacher was Miss Kliner and all the kids described her an a cranky old maid. Renell knew Miss Kliner had to be at least seventy-five years old. She had seen her new teacher plenty of times on the school grounds and she never saw a smile on her face. As the class marched down the hall, Miss Kliner stopped the students and instructed them to get into a straight line. Renell started to cry. As she looked around, she saw tears in the eyes of some of the other girls as well. Before they entered the classroom, Miss Kliner said, "When you find your name on the desk, please be seated." But she did not say that in a mean way and Renell stopped crying.

As always, Renell knew that she would find her name on the front row. After the children were seated, Miss Kliner went over the class rules. Not a peep could be heard in the class. The rules were just about the same as the year before and Renell was used to following directions. That was not hard to do. Next, everyone was instructed to take the books out of the desk and write their name on the appropriare line. Miss Kliner instructed the class not to write in the book, not to fold the pages, not to tear any pages or lose the book because the student's parents would pay for it if anything happened to the book. Renell again had a subdued look on her face and she felt the tears once again running down her face. All she wanted to do was go home! She had never felt that way at school. She loved school!

Lunch did not come fast enough for the entire class. Miss Kliner walked them to the cafeteria in one single file line. Not one person was out of line. It was like night and day when they entered the cafeteria, however. Big welcoming smiles were on the faces of all the cafeteria staff. That really made Renell's day! The staff loaded the children's plates with generous portions of food. The class was allowed to talk softly to the person sitting next to them. After all the children in the class were served, Miss Kliner went to eat her lunch at the teacher's table. All the teachers sat at angles to see their classes.

The classmates Renell spoke to at lunch all stated that they wished the afternoon would go better than the morning and they all agreed that they were going to do everything that Miss Kliner instructed them to do the very first time. They did not want to make her upset. Renell and her classmates also admitted that they were afraid of Miss Kliner and wished that she would smile. A smile would make each of them feel so much better.

The afternoon of that first day of school was a little better. Each student was asked to share what they did over the summer. Many of the students visited grandparents, aunts, uncles and other relatives. One of the students, Rosie, traveled out of the country to visit family in Europe. Wow, that seemed so far away! The farthest Renell had travelled was Alabama and that was by car, not by airplane. She really wanted to know more about Rosie's trip to Europe. She loved the book that Miss Duncan, her second grade teacher, read to the class called *Heidi and the Swiss Alps*, and she really wanted to go to Switzerland some day and climb that mountain.

At three o'clock, the bell rang for the children to go home. Renell wanted to run out of the classroom as fast as she could, but she and the entire class waited to find out the correct and proper procedure to follow in exiting the room after the last bell of the day sounded. Miss Kliner did not go over the exiting bell when she went over the rules at the beginning of class. The students in Renell's class were dismissed by rows, but once they were out of the building, they began shouting to other students on the basketball court. Renell's friends who were assigned the teacher that Renell really wanted had a wonderful first day of school. Renell knew this to be true when her friends came out of their class smiling and stating what a great day they had experienced!

After the conclusion of her first day of school. Renell just wanted to be alone, so she began running up the street. As she ran past the mothers standing outside their homes waiting for their children, each one wanted to know how the first day of school had gone. When Renell just looked at them and didn't respond, all of them wondered what had happened at school because that was not the Renell they knew. The Renell they knew was always talkative and bubbly. Renell knew her mother would talk to them later. If she opened her mouth, Renell knew she would start crying. She just wanted to see her mom. In her haste to get home, however, Renell forgot that her mother was going to pick up her brother and would then stop by Renell's class to introduce herself to Renell's teacher, Miss Kliner. When Renell opened the door and her mom was not there to greet her, she started crying uncontrollably. Finally, when her mother and Steven entered the house, Renell ran into her mother's arms and sobbed and sobbed.

Mrs. Adams comforted her and told her it was going to be a great year. She also said, "Baby, God has all things in control." She stopped crying because of her mom's trust in God, but she felt deep down inside her mom didn't truly understand how she really felt. Her teacher did not smile or say nice things to her that day. She was also a *little afraid of Miss Kliner. Who would really understand this?*

In addition to her challenges regarding her new teacher, Renell could sense that her mother did not look like she was feeling well. She attributed it to one of those days that she was missing Donald.

Renell did not know that her mother was sick. Renell was so sorry for telling her mother about her teacher and she decided not to tell her again. She was just going to keep that feeling to herself. When she asked her mom if she was okay, Mrs. Adams replied, "I know the Lord has not put more on me than I can bear." Renell would later ask her grandmother what that meant. She did not want her mom unhappy about anything, especially how Renell felt about her teacher.

September went by swiftly, and Renell was elated because her prayer that school would go by quick seemed to be answered. The days seemed to fly by. Miss Kliner taught Renell's class new and interesting things, but without a smile. One significant thing happened during a health lesson. For much of her young life, Renell had sucked two fingers in private, usually around her family. Miss Kliner was teaching a lesson about "hitchhike germs." Miss Kliner told the class that some small germs called bacteria live on each small square of their hands, also underneath their fingernails, and between their fingers. She stated that those small bacteria could only be observed under a high-powered microscope. Each time Renell and her classmates touched something the bacteria attached themselves to their fingers, which was the reason for their name, "hitchhike germs." Miss Kliner went on to explain that when Renell and her classmates suck their fingers, the bacteria in their mouths and the germs become little bugs they suck. That frightened Renell so much that she never sucked her fingers again. She got a sick feeling in her stomach thinking about all the little bugs she had eaten. Each night before she stopped sucking her fingers, her fingers would look all shriveled up. No more shriveled fingers! Her family was so happy knowing she had stopped sucking her fingers. They had tried everything others told them would be a remedy to help her stop sucking her two fingers, but nothing had ever worked before.

Renell enjoyed learning and during the previous summer, she memorized all her multiplication tables through to twelve. She used that skill in working at her grandmother's store. Long division was something she was eager to learn. Her sister told her that division was the opposite of multiplication, just as subtraction was the opposite of addition, and that long division was the next step in division.

Throughout the summer and into the school year, Renell continued to love reading. Some of her favorite books were the Nancy Drew detective series and the Boxcar Children series, which consisted of nineteen different books. Each story of the Boxcar Children was centered on the adventures of the four orphaned children who created a home for themselves in an abandoned boxcar in the woods. Intrigued by their story, Renell wanted her parents to take her on a train ride to Crestline to visit her great-grandmother so she could visualize living in a boxcar.

Studying social studies was the subject that most interested Renell. Knowledge about people, how they lived, where and how they worked and how they survived all over the world were questions that baffled Renell. She wanted to use that big globe in the classroom and discover more about all the lines on it. Renell enjoyed reading road maps and trying to use the distance scale. Mr. Adams and Uncle Winston taught her that fun skill. They both agreed that Renell was a good navigator.

One subject she did not particularly like was science. Renell did not like bugs, insects, rodents, and cats. Her brother Steven said, "Science is intriguing! There are so many exciting and fascinating things to learn, pursue, and explore through experiments and observation." Renell wished she could trade places with him when they studied science in her class.

The climate was changing, and fall had made its entrance in a forceful way. Many mornings were crisp and chilly, and sweaters and jackets were needed. October was going to be a fun-filled month with lots of fun activities planned for the children at school and the community. One of the activities was the fall carnival, which was held at Liberty Park. Another fall favorite activity was Halloween, especially trick or treat night. The children would go up and down Oakenwaldt Avenue, knocking on the doors of their many neighbors, who would fill their bags with lots of candy. Renell looked forward to all the fall happenings and she hoped that all of these fun events would be scheduled on Saturday, since Friday night was a church night and the family went to church.

The health and science lessons taught at Renell's school in October focused on the bones in the body, on fire prevention and on staying safe while outside. The class sang songs about the body and were reminded to always wash their hands and keep their fingers out of their mouths. Renell smiled because she had stopped that terrible habit, and she was not putting those "hitchhike germs" in her mouth. She often wondered why she started sucking her fingers in the first place. Her mother and others shared that they felt it was because Steven was born exactly one year and one week after her. She just needed to be the baby a little longer, and she wanted to suck his bottle. Hearing it repeatedly still made Renell laugh. She was so elated that she no longer sucked her fingers!

While the children enjoyed the October carnival, an unforeseen event suddenly happened at the same time in the Adams home. Renell's mother, Mrs. Adams was admitted the hospital for testing to find out why her cough continued to linger. After many tests, Mr. Adams and his family received the devastating news that Mrs. Adams had been diagnosed with pulmonary tuberculosis. What a shock, what a blow! The entire family was in a state of disbelief! After hearing the news, Mrs. Adams remained resolute and unwavering and declared that she trusted the Lord for her healing and deliverance. Even though the family was educated about the disease, numerous questions raced through Renell's mind. She knew that what her parents and others told her meant that her mother's illness was very serious. And Renell knew that the only thing she wanted, more than anything else in the world, was for her mother to be well.

The doctor discussed different options with Mr. and Mrs. Adams to think about concerning her health. He informed them about a fairly new surgery that would remove all or part of a lung to stop the spread of the disease. He felt Mrs. Adams would be a good candidate for the surgery, but he emphasized that all surgeries have risks. The doctor would do whatever Mr. and Mrs. Adams decided. He wanted them to think about the possible options and discuss it with their family. To the best of their ability, Mr. and Mrs. Adams explained the surgical procedure to their family. It was a risk, but they only had two choices—either have the surgery or remain in a sanatorium until she was healed. The doctor told Mrs. Adams that she could be in the sanatorium for years. Renell's mother wanted to go home and be with her family.

Renell prayed each morning and night for her mom. The surgery was performed the week of Halloween. The surgery was successful. The doctor explained the recovery period to Mr. Adams, Mama Jones, and Auntie. For the first few days after the surgery, Renell's mother continued to do relatively well. However, on Halloween evening, she made a sudden turn for the worse. Mr. Adams, Auntie and Uncle Winston were abruptly called to the hospital. The doctor informed them that that Mrs. Adams was experiencing complications with her kidney and that her vital signs were not good.

"Why is this happening?" Mr. Adams frantically asked the doctor and nurses. But no one could answer his question. Mr. Adams and Mrs. Adams' sister broke down and cried when told the grim news that Mrs. Adams would not survive the night. As they gathered closely by her hospital bedside, Mrs. Adams spoke to them softy and whispered her final words. "I love you, honey, I love you, Inell, and Winston. Keep the children together, make sure they finish school and go to college. Keep my babies in church and let them know how much I loved them." As Mr. Adams and her sister, Inell, held her hands and Mr. Adams kissed her, Mrs. Adams stopped breathing. Deep, intense emotion and unspeakable grief filled the hospital room.

Mr. Adams, Auntie and Uncle Winston stayed with Mrs. Adams until the mortician came and picked up Mrs. Adams body. When Mr. Adams returned home, Mama Jones, Renell's grandmother, was still at the Adams' home, babysitting Eugene, Renell and Steven. Prior to their arrival home, Mama Jones had received the news that her daughter had died. Grief stricken, she was taking it very hard. After going out to trick-or-treat several hours earlier, the children had retired and were now sound asleep. The only one who knew what had happened was Renell's older sister, Yvonne, who had been babysitting Tony. When Yvonne found out, she cried the entire night. She could not believe what had happened, that her mother was dead, gone, and that meant she would never ever be with the family again. This was all too familiar. (Memories of Yvonne's late brother, Donald, flooded her thoughts). Yvonne did not look forward to seeing her siblings once they were told the devastating, shocking news about their mom's passing. She knew the next day was going to be a traumatic and heart wrenching day in the Adams' home.

Yvonne did not want her brothers and sister to feel the pain that she was experiencing deep down in her soul and heart. All she could do was cry and pray, cry and pray. She kept thinking, *I will never be with my mom again, I will never see that loving smile, hear those prayers of covering over her children, family, friends and the church.* The pain was excruciating, and she felt like her heart was coming out of her body. Why was this happening again to her family? She wondered where Jesus was in this situation. How was her family going to go forward without her mom? She spent the night at her aunt and uncle's house. She just did not want to see the pain in her father's and siblings' eyes. It was just too much for her to handle.

The next morning, the house filled with relatives and members from the church. Mr. Adams had not slept the entire night. Instead, he cried on and off throughout the entire night. His sisters were there to comfort him and Mama Jones, Mrs. Adams' mother. Mr. Adams prayed and asked the Lord for direction on how to break the overwhelming news to his children. Mrs. Adams' brother and cousin drove the two and a half hours to break the news to Lewis. This was going to be a very emotional experience for all of them. After breaking the news and comforting Lewis to the best of their ability, they went to the college administration office to share the news. The dean assured them that each of Lewis' professors would be notified of the news, and he would be given ample time to complete his assignment. They expressed their condolences and concern for the family and told them to make sure Lewis took as much time as needed before returning back to class. The ride home was somber and depressing. Lewis knew about the surgery, but the last report he had received had been a good one concerning his mom. Mr. Adams wanted to travel to Lewis' college to pick him up and tell him of his mother's passing, but Mr. Adams also knew that he was the only person who could break the sad and devastating news to Eugene, Renell and Steven. Though he knew that the news of Mrs. Adams' passing was going to be overwhelming for Lewis, Mr. Adams also knew that he was in no shape to try and drive the long road to Wilberforce Ohio. All the children were so very close to their mother. She was their encourager, cheerleader, comforter, prayer warrior, and disciplinarian.

Eugene was the first of the three to awaken. He heard people talking in the living room and wondered what was going on. Mr. Adams and their grandmother, Mama Jones, broke the news to him. He could not believe what he was told and asked them to repeat what they just said to him. When they said it the second time, he screamed and burst out crying uncontrollably and shouting in disbelief, "This isn't possible! It's not fair! We just lost Donald, now Mom! Why did this horrible thing happen to my mom?"

Everyone who was in the house, who heard Eugene's heart wrenching cries also began crying as well. It was hard hearing a child cry and cry and be unable to comfort him. Mr. Adams hugged him and told Eugene he could not answer his question and that he wanted to know the very same thing. Eugene went to his room and stated that he wanted to be alone. He didn't want to talk to anyone in the house. Mr. Adams asked him if he would let him know when Renell and Steven woke up if he heard them. He said he would and continued to cry.

Shortly thereafter, Renell woke up and heard Eugene crying. She went into his room and asked, "Eugene, did you lose your lunch money? If you did, I have some money in my bank." Eugene just looked at his sister, continued crying, but left out of his bedroom to tell Mr. Adams that Renell had awakened. When Mr. Adams came into her bedroom, Renell was totally confused. This was a school day and her daddy was always at work when she and her siblings left for school, unless it was a holiday. When her dad entered her room, Renell saw tears in his eyes and she knew something dreadful was going on. Mr. Adams sat on her bed and hugged and squeezed Renell hard. He started crying and told her the sad news about her mother.

Renell screamed and said, "No, no, not Mommy! Lord, please don't let this be true." She felt a stabbing pain in her heart.

"This all had to be a dream," Renell kept saying to herself over and over again. She started shaking all over, and her grandmother came into the room to be with her. Renell repeated over and over, "It just can't be true!" Renell wanted her grandmother to confirm that it wasn't true, that her mother wasn't gone! But Renell looked up to see the tears in her grandmother's eye and she knew it was true.

What were Renell and the other members of her family going to do without her mom? Just those days she had been in the hospital had been so lonely! Mrs. Adams was always home when Renell came through the front door from school. She had their snacks ready and would take some time to talk with them and to intently listen about their day in school. She would then give them a few minutes to wind down before starting their homework. Who would do all that now? Renell began crying again. She no longer wanted to stay in the house and asked if she could go to school. No one in the family wanted her to go, but when she kept saying, "I don't want to stay in the house," Renell's grandmother helped her get ready. And, with that, off to school, Renell went. Steven did not want to go to school, so he stayed home.

When Renell entered her classroom, she told her teacher that her mother had died last night. Miss Kliner just looked at her and Renell went to her seat. What kind of person was her teacher, thought Renell, to not console or says something to make her feel better? The class went on as usual that morning. However, when the class went to lunch, many of the children started asking Renell about her mom. Always, after lunch, the children would go outside for recess if the weather was nice. As soon as her class was dismissed to go outside, Renell left the school and ran up the street to her house. She cried all the way home. When she entered the house, she ran into her father's arms. Renell cried, "Dad, you were right. I should not have gone to school. So many people kept asking me questions about mommy and how she died." Renell was so happy to see her brother Lewis. He hugged her and told her he was happy to see her. He promised her that they would get though this difficult time of their mother's loss together. At that moment, Renell did not ever want to go back to school.

After Renell left the school grounds and came home, her grandmother called the school and spoke with the secretary. Her grandmother then fixed Renell something to eat. Renell was grateful because she could not eat her breakfast and she did not eat her lunch at school because she felt so bad. But once the food her grandmother prepared was in front of her on the table, she suddenly could not eat. Renell was no longer hungry. Her taste and desire for food seemed to have vanished. Her siblings told her their appetite was also gone.

The rest of the day, Renell sat in her room perusing through many of the family photo albums of her mom, dad and her siblings. The tears kept flowing until she went to sleep. Different family members kept checking on her. Each time she heard them outside of her door, she pretended that she was asleep. She didn't want to talk. She only wanted her mom! Her father knew that Renell was not asleep. Each night the family always said good night and prayed together.

Each night the Adams family always said good night and prayed together. This night would be no different. Steven came into Renell's room and told her their father wanted Renell and her siblings to come to their parents' bedroom. All the children sat on the bed and Mr. Adams told them how much he loved them. He shared their mother's final words and he assured them they would get through the devastating loss of their mother. Steven told his dad that he wanted to sleep in his room. Mr. Adams hugged him and told him he could sleep in the room until he was ready to go and sleep in his own bedroom. The grieving father hugged and kissed his now motherless children and they prayed a far different prayer than the family had ever prayed before!

Renell didn't sleep well that night. She kept waking up, listening for her mother's voice, saying "It's time to get up." Renell would lift her head off the pillow and remember what had happened the day before. Her mother would never return. And then Renell would remember what had happened the day before. Her mother would never return, and she began crying more. She wanted to go to her parents' room, but Renell thought she would awaken her father and brother. This was not a dream but reality. Life was already different.

Fear set in, and Renell began questioning in her mind, Lord, who will be next in the family to pass? Eight years old was no longer a fun time anymore. Instead, she had so many questions, especially, *where was God?* Her father, grandmother, aunt and others could not answer her question, where was God, though they tried to steadfastly reassure her that the Lord loved her and all of them very much.

Nighttime was the hardest because Renell would dream that her mother was still in the house. Many nights she cried herself to sleep, knowing she would never ever see her precious mother again. So many people meant well, but they just did not understand what was going on in Renell's mind. In the middle of the night, Renell would awaken to hear her mother's voice echo in her mind, "Good, better, best! Never let it rest! Until the good is better and the better is best."

Life was totally different and would never be the same. Eight-year-old Renell of Oakenwaldt Avenue believed with God's help, someway, somehow, joy would one day return to the Adams' home! Most of all, a part of her mother would always be with her!

About the Illustrator

 Jason Elisha Brown was born on January 26, 1995, in Richmond, Virginia, to William and Debra Brown. At the tender age of seven years old, his parents knew that he was gifted in drawing when he left all the evidence of his artistic work conspicuously displayed on a wall and on a chair. In middle school, Jason won first place in a Martin Luther King Jr. art competition, sponsored by the North Carolina Association of Teachers. In high school, Jason painted a mural for a dentist's office. Jason also enjoyed a graphic design class at Fayetteville Technical Community College.

Art has always been therapeutic for Jason, and it has been a way for him to express his feelings, thoughts, and creative gift. He also enjoys calligraphy, forming strokes of art at the touch of a pen and paper, painting, mixing colors and the utilization of different brush strokes—all to achieve an amazing, creative design. With his creative ability, Jason can make a blank sheet of paper or canvas come to vivid life.

About the Author

 Muriel Renell Allen Brooks is a native of Mansfield, Ohio, who grew up on Oakenwaldt Avenue. She is the wife of Robert Lewis Brooks, a retired US Army Vietnam War veteran and the mother of two adult sons, Robert Lewis II and Marc (Suranda) and grandmother to four grandchildren, Yasmeen, Bryce, Jaidyn, Xavier, one great-grandson, Braylen, and Kimberly Webb (Jaidyn's mother).

As a child, Muriel enjoyed the company of older people and loved to ask them questions about their lives as children. She also loved playing jacks, climbing trees playing house and playing school with friends. Muriel was often the teacher and the front porch of her family's home, the schoolroom.

After graduation from college with a bachelor's degree in elementary education, Muriel became a teacher. She later earned a master's degree in education. Out of her thirty-four years as a teacher, Muriel spent thirty of those years with the Department of Defense, teaching military children in the United States and Germany. She loved her students and always wanted the best for each of them. Muriel and her son, Marc, formed All in One Consulting, LLC, in which Muriel served as an educational consultant.

For Muriel, her Lord and Savior, Jesus Christ, is number one in her life. She is a member of Bethel Christian Assembly, led by her pastor Bishop Jerry Swinney and his wife, Lady Frances Swinney. Muriel remains actively involved in several ministries in her church. She is one of the directors of the children's church, Kingdom Heritage, is an adult Sunday school teacher, serves on the altar ministry and is an active member in the ladies' ministry. Muriel is also a member of

R.O.C.K (Resourceful Opportunities of the Christian Kingdom), a networking group of business owners at her church. Additionally, Muriel serves as president of the Gateway of H.O.P.E., is a member of Pathways for Prosperity in Fayetteville, North Carolina. Muriel serves on the North Carolina K-12 grade education committee and has been a member of the NAACP since the tender age of ten years old. Lastly, Muriel volunteers for the **Army Community Services** on Fort Bragg, North Carolina.